Life in an American Denmark

by

Alfred C. Nielsen

With an Introduction by
Dr. Philip H. Person

Give me a simple life, a merry heart,
And kings may keep their pomp and garments splendid;
Let me in hut and mansion live the part
Of one from worthy ancestors descended,
With eye for things above as God ordained,
Awake to greatness, goodness, truth and beauty,
Yet knowing well the yearnings unattained,
Through knowledge, great achievement, deeds and duty.

N. F. S. GRUNDTVIG.
Translated by S. D. Rodholm.
Copyright D. A. Y. P. L.

Bookstore
Grand View College
Des Moines 16, Iowa

Price $2.50

TO FATHER, MOTHER,
HELEN AND CARL

Copyright 1962 by Alfred C. Nielsen

PRINTED BY
AMERICAN PUBLISHING COMPANY
ASKOV, MINNESOTA
1962

CONTENTS

Introduction

Author's Note

Chapter:

LIST OF ILLUSTRATIONS

Father and Mother, 1879
The First Nysted Church
The Folk School, About 1910
Pastor and Mrs. Thorvald Knudsen
Pastor and Mrs. C. P. Hoiberg
The C. P. Hoiberg Tombstone

INTRODUCTION

The Immigrant Tide to the United States has been ebbing ever since restrictive legislation was passed at the close of the First World War. The various nuclei of nationality groups that settled mostly in the northern part of the United States have been slowly dissolving and losing their identity both in custom and language. The percentage of foreign born in our cities and rural places has been going down for forty years. And with this process the fear of the "alien" has largely disappeared.

Many had feared that these foreign born communities would lead to a divided country. The counsel of Jane Addams of Hull House was ignored. She contended that these clusters of foreign born people were a necessity; that they acted as a "bridge of understanding" over which the foreign born could more easily pass into the larger American life. Documents like this one prove how right and wise she was.

The day of "Immigrant literature" is probably over. The immigrant press has been receding since the turn of the century. Biographies by immigrants such as: Steiner, Pannunzio, Bok, Lewisohn, Pupin, Adamic and many others, have dwindled to a trickle. We have come to the end of the era of the immigrant.

However, the children of the immigrant have a different and significant story to tell, compared to their forebears. They were really living in two cultures instead of essentially one. Theirs was a problem of assimilation whereas their parents had the problem of accommodation. Thus the immigrant's children, with one foot in each of the cultures tended to become, as the late Louis Adamic has pointed out, critical in their attitudes. They were pushed from two sides to accept cultural values which were in some cases in diametric opposition. Some, of course, tended to reject one or the other, and they became either super-patriots or were accused of being hyphenated Americans. Some even became ashamed of their immigrant origin.

The author of this treatise took the course followed by most immigrant's children. He tried to preserve and integrate the higher values of his Danish background and his American heritage. He became an excellent and much beloved teacher in the social science field. Thousands of young people through the years have benefited by his critical analyses and his understanding heart. These students and members of his lecture audiences are to be found in every state of the Union and in some foreign countries. And the welcome mat is always out for "A. C." wherever he goes.

The author's background included a wide knowledge and appreciation of the Danish Folk School system and its founder, Bishop Grundtvig. He spent seven years of his earlier life taking work and teaching in such institutions as had been transplanted in this country in Nebraska, Iowa and Minnesota. The last part of his teaching career — over twenty years — was spent in Grand View College in Des Moines, as Instructor, Dean and President. This college was in the same tradition as the Danish Folk High Schools. He had high hopes that this system could somehow make a contribution to the secondary schools of this country, and to the Junior Colleges as well. No one, I think, would deny that our high schools need improvement, and in time, his hopes for this improvement may come.

I first met Alfred Nielsen in a Central Nebraska Teachers' College in 1915. Through the years we have spent many hours discussing subjects such as the theme of this book. Both of us were children of immigrants. Both of us grew up in nationality groups in rural Nebraska. Both of us became college teachers in the social science field. However, Alfred is Danish and I am Swedish. To the uninitiated, this should make for conflict rather than harmony. But, after all, we are both Scandinavians! True, one of our chief delights has been — and still is — to dredge up or to fabricate stories that put the other's nationality in the position of being crude, or stupid, or worse. But this is only to add savor to the sauce of living. Perhaps only Scandinavians would understand this.

We should have many more documents such as this one, written and preserved. The children of the immigrants of the 1870s and '80s are growing old. Unless more of them leave such records, the history of this phase of our country's growth will suffer. Their children and grandchildren should be able to read and to understand, and to be proud of the struggles and contributions made by their forebears, even though they themselves have integrated American personalities that have been nurtured by a multiplicity of nationality backgrounds.

> PHILIP H. PERSON,
> Emeritus Professor,
> University of Wisconsin, Milwaukee.

AUTHOR'S NOTE

In writing this story, I have relied upon some notes left by my father, some notes of my own and conversations with many people, especially my sister, Anna, and my brother, Christian. Mr. Thomas Hermansen of Marquette, Nebraska, Mrs. Agnes Lauritsen of Alma, Nebraska, Mr. F. Clarey Nielsen of Centuria, Wisconsin, Mr. Willie Nielsen of St. Paul, Nebraska, and Mrs. Harriet Price of Dannebrog, Nebraska, have given me valuable information.

The following people have read the manuscript: Dr. and Mrs. Harald Jensen of St. Paul, Minnesota; the Rev. Enok Mortensen of Des Moines, Iowa; Mr. and Mrs. N. C. Nielsen of Des Moines; Dr. and Mrs. P. H. Person of Milwaukee, Wisconsin; and Mr. Dan Williams, Director of the Des Moines Public Library. I want to thank all these people for valuable suggestions.

> ALFRED C. NIELSEN,
> Des Moines, Iowa
> September 1, 1962

I

WHY THEY LEFT EUROPE

Fifty million souls, mostly young people, left Europe between 1820 and 1920, and most of them came to the United States. There were many reasons for this emigration and surely two of the chief ones were: poverty and the curse of war. Between 1700 and 1800 the countries of Europe fought these destructive wars: The War of Spanish Succession, the Great Northern War, the War of Austrian Succession, the Seven Years' War, the Wars of the French Revolutions, and several minor ones.

In 1775 the American colonies rose up against the mother country, England. It was in that year that the embattled farmers at Concord and Lexington fired a shot heard round the world. In 1776 Thomas Jefferson wrote the Declaration of Independence and that, too, was heard round the world.

Young enthusiasts from Europe came to help George Washington in the struggle for freedom. Among them were such men as Thomas Paine, Lafayette, Pulaski and von Steuben.

In 1789 the French Revolution began. It was not only heard round the world, it shocked the world. It began slowly and orderly enough and then took on momentum till most of Europe was involved; and before it was over there was fighting in the New World.

France, like the United States, became a republic. The stupid French king, Louis XVI, was executed and his sweet and silly little wife, Marie Antoinette, went the same way. The new France fought civil wars at home and wars of liberation abroad. A man on horseback, Napoleon, arose and he won military victories from Moscow to Madrid.

7

In 1803 President Thomas Jefferson bought an empire, Louisiana, from Napoleon and that without firing a shot. Jefferson had long been interested in the West. He thought farming was the best way of life and here was land for his beloved farmers. However, he was not quite certain about the boundaries of his new empire, so he sent Lewis and Clark out to see and explore. They went as far west as the Pacific Ocean.

In 1815 Napoleon fought and lost his last battle. To make sure that he would cause no further disturbance, the leaders of Europe sent him to St. Helena.

At the Congress of Vienna old Europe met to put the continent together again, and to make Europe safe from "French ideas." To this end they set up the Holy Alliance.

For some years this policy of repression seemed to succeed. The smart leaders were sure they could stop ideas with bullets. When a political fire broke out in Spain, a French army put it out. Priests, bishops and nobles were restored to their proper places. The Spanish expedition was so successful that Great Britain was afraid that another expedition might be sent to the New World to restore rebellious colonies in Latin America to Spain. This would interfere with British trade, so Foreign Minister Canning suggested that Great Britain and the United States go together to hinder such an expedition. This led to the Monroe Doctrine.

When an uprising took place in Italy, the Austrian army was sent in to restore order and to put a stop to subversive ideas.

There was trouble in Germany too. It was feared that some professors and students in universities had gotten "French ideas," and soon Austria filled German universities with spies to see that nothing controversial was discussed and to see that libraries contained nothing but safe and dull books.

Louis XVIII had become king of France after the fall of Napoleon, and believe it or not, here was a Bourbon king who had learned something. He knew he would have to behave himself lest he lose his head or go travelling again.

8

Unfortunately he was not immortal. He went to his reward in 1824 and was succeeded by his brother, Charles X. Here was a true son of the celebrated Bourbon line. He had learned nothing and had forgotten nothing. He began a policy of repression and soon had a host of enemies. In July 1830 the lid blew off and this brave king fled the land. His place was taken by Louis Philippe, the Citizen King.

When the Poles heard the glad tidings that a new revolution had broken out in France, they rose. When Czar Nicholas heard that his Polish subjects had shown their ingratitude toward him by an uprising, he told his soldiers to saddle their horses and gallop off to Poland and teach the Poles how to die. They did just that. The Polish revolt was crushed cruelly, and there were sighs and cries along the Vistula River.

Belgium had been handed over to the Netherlands at the Vienna Congress and when the Belgians heard of the revolution in France, they rose too. The leaders of the Dutch were told by the French and the British that they had better not go too far in repressing the Belgians and Belgium won its independence.

In Germany and Italy there were disturbances again and these too were put down.

There was no peace in Europe. All the time it seemed there were wars or threats of war.

In America the people had been able to settle their political problems with ballots. Two years before the French July Revolution, Andrew Jackson had led his triumphant hosts to victory and the Jacksonian era brought in a number of reforms. But on the European continent it seemed that the only way for the masses to win any victories was with bullets.

It was perhaps Metternich who said that when France has a cold, all of Europe sneezes. Well, in 1848 France had another cold and Europe really did sneeze. This time the French masses rose and drove out King Louis Philippe and the short-lived Second French Republic was born and soon the bullets were flying over much of Europe.

9

Timid souls were convinced that this was the beginning of the end. In France, Germany, Bohemia, Austria, Hungary and Italy armies marched and blood ran in the streets. Little Denmark was an exception. When the multitude asked the good King, Frederick VII, for a constitution, he gave them one and there was no uprising. But there were uprisings in Germany, Bohemia, Austria, Italy and Hungary. They were crushed and in the latter country with the help of the Russian army, as in 1956, and the Hungarian patriot, Kossuth, fled. Later he came to the United States where he was received with wild enthusiasm.

Thousands of liberals now gave up. There was no hope for freedom in Europe. For the little man, there was nothing but repression, war and poverty.

During 1845 and 1846 came the Irish Potato famine. This was due to the failure of the potato crop which was the principal food for these poor people and thousands died of starvation. In a wild panic hordes of people sought relief in flight. One gate was open to them and that was America.

Before the forties immigration into the United States had been light. In the fifty-five years before 1845, fewer immigrants landed on our shores than came during the last five years of the forties. In 1850, 310,000 came.

During the forties most of the immigrants came from Ireland and Germany. From the former they came, of course, because of hunger; and from the latter it was due to political discontent. Most of the Irish remained in the larger eastern cities, while the Germans went farther west.

Two things should be mentioned that stirred the minds of the poor and ambitious in western Europe. One was the discovery of gold in California in 1848. California became the land of gold and adventure. The other was the passage of the Homestead Act by the U. S. Congress in 1862. Soon the little people all over Europe were talking about this new land of opportunity where a man with courage and willing hands could get a farm for a song. And interestingly, in the nineteenth century, the governments were glad to see their political dissenters leave the country. They did not build walls to keep them in or refuse them passage. So they said good-bye to Europe. Thousands, yes millions left for the United States. Among them were my parents.

It was in 1953 that I visited Denmark for the first time. My father, Rasmus B. Nielsen, was born in that country on August 4, 1851. My father was a good story teller. As I rode that bus west on a beautiful spring morning, from the city of Aarhus in Jutland, the bus driver announced the names of the villages as we came to them. Here were the names of the towns that father had mentioned in his stories: Laasby, Galten, Skørring and Mollerup. A thousand memories from the life of father came to my mind. Presently the bus driver told us that we were in the village of Mollerup. This was the place where my father was born. My cousin, Anna Moller, met me at the station and bade me welcome to the home of my father.

My father's parents were Niels Christensen and Karen Marie. While father was still very young, about five years of age, a sister was born. This child was sickly and contracted a contagious disease, and father was sent to his grandparents in Skørring, where he lived for many years. This village was about five miles from his home. Not long after moving to Skørring, this sister died. His grandparents were Mr. and Mrs. Rasmussen and they had a good farm at this village. I have visited this place many times and it is a lovely community.

His grandparents were kind to him. His grandfather was a good story teller and took him along on long walks through the fields. Father early liked to sing and his grandfather was proud of this ability in his grandson.

When father was about ten years old, his grandfather died suddenly from a heart attack. The management of the farm now fell to his son, Mikkel Rasmussen, who was father's uncle. His uncle was a capable person, but father missed the kindness of his grandfather.

For some time father was the herd boy and as such took care of the cattle and ran errands for the older people about

11

the farm. This work was often neither easy nor pleasant.

Father was confirmed when he was fourteen. He recalled that he got a new suit of clothes for the occasion, but he had to wear his uncle's shoes. He begged for a pair of new shoes. He cried, but got none. He told himself that if his grandfather had lived he would have had new shoes with his new clothes.

Some time later his uncle married a rather wealthy girl and there was more luxury in this farm home. Her name was Karen Bolette. Father continued to work for them. A son, Rasmus Knudsen, was born to them, and he and father in time became good friends.

When father was about seventeen years of age, his father passed away. For a couple of years his mother wrestled with all the problems that go with a farm loaded with debt. However, in the same village was a widower, who had a good farm and he proposed marriage to the widow. She accepted the good offer and they were married. Her husband's name was Anders Rasmussen. He united the two farms and built new buildings on his wife's farm. The house he built is still in use.

Anders Rasmussen had two boys from his previous marriage. They were Lauritz Bomholt and Rasmus Andersen.

A couple of years after his mother had married again, father was asked to come back home to Mollerup to work on the farm. He did that. He now had two half-brothers with whom to work and play. But it was not long till his mother had more children. They were: Marie, Niels Moller and Anders Rask. It will be clear that in this farm home there were, so to speak, three sets of children: father from an earlier marriage, the two boys that his step-father brought with him, and the three children from the new marriage. According to father's story, all the children got along well with each other. It speaks well for his mother that she kept some harmony in this home.

Father worked on the home farm for some years. During this period he had a hitch in the army, which he liked quite well.

12

It should be mentioned that father seemed to have had a habit of falling in love with women below him in class. A hundred years ago, the people in Denmark were quite class conscious. A girl worked as a milkmaid on the farm, and father fell madly in love with her. Her parents were poor. Both of father's parents were bitterly opposed to this whole affair. A child was born to this poor girl and father frankly admitted that the child was his and wanted to marry the girl. Because of the bitter opposition, this was not done.

After some years father took a job as the head man on a near-by farm. Here he managed the work in the fields. He took the lead in such work as threshing by hand with a flail and cutting grain and hay with a scythe. On this farm, women did the milking, the spinning and the weaving of cloth. Here, too, they had a brewery and a bakery. While father worked at this place the first railway and telegraph were built through this part of Denmark.

On this farm also worked a milkmaid whose name was Gertrude Christensen, my mother. She was pretty and a strong capable worker. But she came from a poor peasant home. I have seen the home in which she was born and it surely was a simple dwelling. Once again father fell in love with a girl below him in class.

Gertrude Christensen was born February 14, 1856, not very far from Mollerup at a place called Dallerup Mark. Her parents were thrifty, hard workers who had a small farm with rather poor soil. They had but few earthly things and many children. Their names were Mathias, Gertrude, Ib, Jorgen, Kirsten and Laus. Four of them, Mathias, Gertrude, Jorgen and Ib, tried their fortune in America.

In this home there were many mouths to feed and bread was dear. Mother went to work for others at the tender age of eight. It was her task to herd geese, and anyone acquainted with the stubborn habits of this fowl know how utterly obnoxious it usually is. In the chilly, rainy weather of Denmark, she was in the field. She froze and she cried and cried, but her tears did not make the geese less cantankerous.

As mentioned above, father met Gertrude and fell in

13

love with her. Once again there were family objections. Father's parents had a large and well-improved farm. Mother's parents had a small farm and they were poor. The barrier between was wide and deep.

At this time Denmark was flooded with literature telling about the wonders of the U. S. A. In America Uncle Sam was rich enough to give every man a farm. Father had had enough of family interference with his love affairs. He and mother decided to try their fortune in America — with or without parental blessings. Father would leave first to find a place to live. When he had found that, mother would follow him. In fairness it should be mentioned that when my parents announced their engagement and their plan to leave for America, the shock was great. However, father's parents had been impressed with mother's ability as a worker and finally gave the young people their blessings.

II

TO THE NEW WORLD

In the spring of 1878 father left for America. An agent of the Union Pacific Railway was in Denmark and had convinced a number of Danes that they should try their luck in America. This agent was a Dane and since the Union Pacific had much land in Nebraska, he told of the wonders of that state. According to him, Howard County was a veritable Garden of Eden and he convinced father and others that that was the place to go. They had almost no facts as to climate or soil. I have forgotten most of what father told me about his journey to America. I do know that they went by way of Glasgow, Scotland. The voyage across the Atlantic was no luxury. They landed at Castle Garden in New York. From there the group took an immigrant train west. They did not take a sleeper and finally became dead tired. One night a pick-pocket went through the car and father lost his billfold. Fortunately he had concealed most of his money in an improvised pocket in his underwear. Grand Island, Nebraska was their railway destination. Tired and dirty they finally arrived there.

A Danish colony had been founded in Howard County in 1871. A group of young Danes from Wisconsin had found a spot near the mouth of Oak Creek. They chose this place because the soil was good and there was much timber along Oak Creek and some along the Middle Loup River. The leader of this undertaking was a Mr. Lars Hannibal. He was perhaps an agent of the Union Pacific Railway. Under the terms of the government contract, this railway owned considerable land in Howard County and the railway naturally wanted settlers, and hard working immigrants would be ideal for this pioneer work.

The Danes began to arrive in 1871. The first two white women in Howard County were Mrs. Lars Hannibal and Mrs. Laerke Sorensen. Mrs. Sorensen I have known. The village of Dannebrog was founded. Dannebrog is the name of the Danish flag, the oldest flag in the world.

In the June 15, 1922, issue of the **Dannebrog News**, P. M. Hannibal, the son of Dannebrog's first postmaster, Lars Hannibal, wrote his impression of the new country: "About two hundred Pawnee Indians camped on the Loup near us and the Sioux not far away. Many wild animals were here. At night we heard the howling and yelping of wolves and coyotes; and in the morning the cackling and crowing of prairie chickens. There were prairie dog towns haunted by owls and rattlesnakes. Antelopes were plenty, wildcats sneaked around; and beavers in the creek were cutting down trees and building dams. Adventure, privation, fun and danger seemed all mixed up from the start; and later the grasshoppers, storms, prairie fires and Indian scares are known in history. The American motto, 'In God We Trust' was our motto too."

Dannebrog is about twenty-five miles northwest of Grand Island. The group of Danish immigrants, who had arrived by train in Grand Island a spring morning in 1878, managed to find wagons going to Dannebrog. Across the prairies, creeks and sand hills they drove. Finally they came to the Middle Loup River. There was no bridge and the water was swift and deep in places, but they did manage to get across.

The people in Dannebrog were glad to see new and prospective settlers. They wanted the colony to grow and there was always a shortage of labor in the new settlement. It should be remembered that when the first Danes arrived in 1871, there was not a road, a bridge or a single building. The amount of work to be done in these new colonies seemed endless. These pioneers needed roads, bridges, houses, barns, granaries, machinery, etc. Money was needed badly and money was even more scarce than labor. The man on the American frontier was usually an inflationist. It was especially the western farmers who were the Greenbackers, Populists and the followers of William Jennings Bryan and his Sixteen to One.

In 1878 Dannebrog was a village with a general store or two and a few primitive houses. The houses were small but the human hearts were big. The new arrivals had no trouble finding food and shelter till each had a job. Father got work on the Niels Nielsen farm some miles northwest of Dannebrog. Niels Nielsen was an interesting person and surely not a conformist. He had arrived some years earlier from Lolland, Denmark. He was a well informed farmer. His son, F. Clarey Nielsen, told me that for many years his father read the **New York World**. He was a leader among his own and a progressive in politics.

So father began to unlearn Danish farming methods and to learn American ways. One little incident comes to my mind. He was plowing one day when he saw a cute, little animal running down the furrow. It was so pretty with its black fur and white stripes that he decided to try to catch it. He stopped short when he found that he was enveloped

16

in the most horrible stench. It was his first experience with the American skunk.

In what free time he had that first summer, he looked about in the settlement for a piece of land. He soon learned that the good homestead land near Dannebrog was gone. There was still school land and railroad land but such land was not free. A friend drove for him as far north as Munson Creek where homestead land was available but he said the country there reminded him of a Siberia. Another friend drove for him to Sherman County but that too looked wild. He was told that a 160-acre farm about four miles northwest of Dannebrog was for sale. The owner lived in Grand Island and father walked the twenty-five miles to see him. Here he learned that a Martin Hermansen had bought that farm a few hours earlier. Later he and Mr. Hermansen became good friends.

Father caught a ride back to Dannebrog where he met Mr. Lars Hannibal who told him that the Union Pacific Railway owned an 80-acre farm about four miles west from Dannebrog and advised him to buy that. This farm was located on Section 5, the same section where the village of Nysted was built later. He paid four dollars an acre for this farm.

Father now wrote to his fiancee and his parents that he had bought a piece of land and would soon build a house — a sod house. When his father heard this, he asked how much it would cost to build a better house. Father replied that it would cost from $250 to $300, and his father sent him the money.

In the fall when he was through working for Niels Nielsen, he began to work for himself. He bought a team of horses and a wagon. Of course, lumber and other building material had to be hauled from Grand Island over a poor trail. By the spring of 1879 a two-room wooden house had been built. He also had a small barn, a small granary and a cow or two — In those days a young man could start farming when he had a thousand dollars. — Now he waited for his sweetheart — Gertrude Christensen.

17

On an early morning in the spring of 1879 a clumsy ocean vessel drew up to the pier of Castle Garden. It came to disgorge its cargo of human beings, immigrants from Europe. Hundreds of them poured out of the steerage, carrying bundles and packages in their hands and on their backs. Among them was a medium-sized young woman with dark brown eyes and pretty features. She smelled of the filthy steerage. Her strange clothes, her many bundles and her foreign tongue marked her at once as an alien. The sophisticated who stood on the pier must have thought of her as another undesirable foreigner. Little could they know that there was deathless music in her soul. This woman was my mother.

While she did not see the Statue of Liberty, she often spoke of it. She was tired and homeless, but she was not hopeless. She was one of the thousands who had fled from Europe; and now she stood on the good, free earth — America.

Father and Mother, 1879

As mentioned earlier, she had gone to work for others at a tender age. How she ever learned to love pretty melodies and good things in a brutal world, I do not know and will never understand.

She came five thousand miles to marry the man of her choice and to build a good home. Five thousand miles is the distance from Denmark to central Nebraska. It took a woman with courage in her heart to do that.

She told me many years later with sorrow in her voice,

that one of her first experiences in America was to be cheated. She knew that it would take the immigrant train many days to reach Nebraska so she bought a food package, but it was rotten. She never told me how many days it took, but she did tell me that the train was very dirty.

Father, of course, met her in Grand Island. They were married there by a civil officer. Father had learned a little of the American language, but she did not understand a word of the questions asked, and had been taught what to reply. This was really faith, hope and love! There were no wedding guests, only a witness. Following the ceremony, father and mother drove in a lumber wagon across the prairies to their new home.

The house was new and small — just two rooms. Father had bought a few pieces of furniture. When she entered her home she found one wedding present. A kind neighbor lady had put a small paper bag of sugar on the table. This lady was Mrs. Jorgen Christensen. That was all. There were no friends to receive her. She knew not a soul except father. What did fate hold in store for her? While she never said a word about it, I know that her sensitive soul must have been filled with emotion.

This was to be her home for the rest of her life. How different from her native Denmark with streams, woods and close neighbors. The nearest neighbor was a half mile away. There was hardly a house or tree to be seen on the endless prairies. At night the awful silence could be broken by the yelp of a coyote. There were frequent storms. In Denmark the weather was usually gentle, but here the flash of lightning, the crash of thunder and the howling winds filled her with fear. She had never experienced anything like the scorching southwest winds in summer or the roaring blizzards in winter.

III

THE NEW PRAIRIE HOME

During many years father hauled what grain he had to sell to Grand Island. He would load the wagon in the evening, get up at three in the morning and set out across the prairies. He drove with horses. They could walk rather fast with a load if it was not too large. Many of the Danish farmers drove with oxen. I knew one of the old timers who hauled his grain to Grand Island with oxen. He told me that his oxen walked so slowly that the wheels on his wagon barely moved. In places the hills were steep and the sand was deep.

When father left home at three, he could, if there were no accidents, be in Grand Island with his load by noon. He had walked most of the way. There were two reasons for walking; one was to keep warm in winter, and the other was to lighten the load for the horses. In the village there was always the burning question of the price of grain. There was also the handicap of language. His English was very poor. All his neighbors and the businessmen in Dannebrog were Danes. During most of the year he had no use for this foreign tongue, but in the presence of Grand Island grain merchants, he really needed a knowledge of the English. He felt that the rascals* cheated him. Like most farmers of those days, he felt that the slick businessman, whom he did not know, cheated him. Some times they paid him as little as forty cents a bushel for his good wheat. Forty cents a bushel, and it seemed to him that he had four hundred bills to pay!

When he had sold his grain and had unloaded, he drove

---

* When the railroad reached St. Paul some years later, the farmers installed their own scale.

to a livery barn to give his horses a feed and a rest. They needed to rest for about three hours. While his horses had their feed and rest, he ate his bread which mother had prepared for him. He usually sat in a sheltered place in the barn. Usually he took a little nap after his cold lunch. At about four or five in the afternoon he set out for home. Usually the wagon was loaded again with such things as lumber or feed.

During the long day, mother had been alone at home. The day had not seemed so long as one would think, since there were so many things to do. There were the usual things about the house, and outside there were the chickens, the pigs, the calves and the cattle. In winter there was always danger of blizzards. She kept an eye on the skies. If it looked like a storm, she would have the animals in shelter before it broke. Always she fed the chickens, the pigs, the calves and the cows. She did the milking and took care of the milk and cream. When all this was done, she settled down to wait for her man. The waiting time was long. From time to time she went outside to listen for the clatter of a wagon. The limitless prairies could be so quiet and it was often near midnight before father came home — hungry and tired. He had worked for at least twenty hours and there was no extra pay for overtime.

If a person has not lived on the prairies of the mid-west, it is not easy to imagine how violent the storms can be. In the summer of 1883, there was promise of a most bountiful harvest. How often had not mother and father walked into the fields of barley and wheat. What a wonderful yield it would be this year. Harvest time came and father and a neighbor had begun to cut the barley. They had cut but a few rounds when mother brought the mid-afternoon lunch. It was a hot, sultry day and father remarked that he did not like the looks of some clouds that were taking shape in the northwest. His neighbor said that this could mean hail. Following the lunch, father drove the harvester another round and then he could see the storm coming. He barely got the horses into the barn when the storm broke with full fury. There was a deafening noise. It was a hailstorm. Mother was in the house. Never had she experienced anything like it. In a minute every window pane in the west and north sides of the house was smashed. In terror she fled to the southeast corner of the house — covering her head with a blanket.

However, prairie hailstorms usually don't last long and this one did not. But how their little world looked. Their little trees had been stripped of their leaves and the wheat and barley had been beaten into the ground. The neighbor remarked, "We sure got finished harvesting in a hurry." The harvest in that part of the Danish settlement was over, but fortunately the swath of the storm was not very wide. There was grain enough for man and beast. Some days later father got a job in the area where there was a good crop.

As the years passed hundreds of Danish immigrants came to the settlement on Oak Creek. Dannebrog grew, roads were laid out, fences were built, houses sprang up here and there and timber claims were planted. For some years the farmers continued to haul their farm produce to Grand Island. It was a great day when the Union Pacific Railway built its road to St. Paul, the county seat of Howard County. Now the farmers of our neighborhood had only twelve — fourteen miles to a railway. Some years later the U. P. built its road through Dannebrog and on to Loup City. Our home was then about four miles from a railway.

While the community grew, the families also grew. It was a community of young people and many children. There were few old people and no clubs for Senior Citizens! In 1880 my oldest sister, Anna, was born. There was no doctor in town and no midwife. A neighbor lady came in to be of what help she could. Mother must have suffered not only physical but also mental agony. But all went well. In 1882 my sister, Marie, was born and again all went well.

At about this time a mid-wife took residence in our community. She was Mrs. Jens Andersen. For many years she attended the birth of hundreds of babies in our

22

community. To my knowledge in all her many years of practice, she did not lose one woman in childbirth.

When my mother felt that she was going to give birth to my brother, Anker, father rushed to the barn at midnight to harness the horses to fetch the mid-wife. Mother had told him that this was a hurry up affair. There was much snow so father hitched the horses to a bobsled. Across the fields he drove as fast as the horses could run. He found Mrs. Andersen at home and soon they were on their way back. There were some rather steep drifts and father had to guide the horses around the worst of them, and up and down went the horses and the sled. Finally father thought the mid-wife had become so quiet, and to his surprise he discovered that he had lost her. In the darkness he could not see her. He traced the tracks back to a large drift and there sat the mid-wife with ruffled dignity, but with no bones broken. She arrived in time to deliver a boy. This was in 1884. Two years later my brother, Christian, was born. In 1889 I was born and in 1892 my twin sisters, Amanda and Agneta, were born. Finally in 1899, the youngest of us all, my brother, Holger, came. How we loved this late arrival! We were now eight children. Mrs. Andersen had attended the birth of all of us except my two older sisters.

All of us children were born at home. During my early childhood we never saw a doctor in our house. When my sister, Marie, broke a leg, my father set it. For many years we lived in the two-room house that father had built before mother arrived. First a small shanty was added. Nine of us lived in this home. We children slept three in a bed. Quite often one of mother's brothers lived with us in the winter time. How mother managed this is surely a mystery to me. The shanty kitchen was so cold in winter that things froze in it. In the morning I would go to the family water pail for a drink to find the dipper frozen solidly in the ice. I begged mother for a drink and I was told that I would have to wait till water could be brought in from the pump.

I am not able to remember the two-room house that our family lived in for some years. However, in 1888 father

23

added the above mentioned shanty to the north end of the house and this I can remember.

In the kitchen was a large wood stove, a large box for wood and cobs, a cupboard for dishes, a table and some straight back chairs. We ate our meals in this kitchen except on Sunday and when we had company.

The next room to the south was a combination dining-living room. Against one wall was a bench and beside this bench was a dining room table. At night this bench could be extended and made into a bed. There was a straw tick in the bottom. Anker, Chris and I slept in this bed. There were two rocking chairs and some more straight back chairs in this room. Near the south wall was a heating stove and near it a box for wood and cobs. There was no rug on the floor and I can still see the wide boards which were painted from time to time. To make this room a bit more cozy, mother had some short ruffled curtains at the top of the windows. In the northwest corner of the room was a floor door which opened to the cellar stairs.

The room to the south was a bedroom. There was a large bed in which mother and father slept. Under it, during the day, was another bed. At night this was hauled out and in it slept Anna and Marie. Against one wall stood a large wardrobe.

The walls in the kitchen were calcimined and those in the two other rooms were covered with wallpaper.

The pump and well were near the house. Water was so important in this semi-arid region. The well was sixty feet deep and had been dug by hand. It was a Danish immigrant who dug the well and he did it so well that it lasted for fifty years.

IV

EARLY CHURCH AND FOLK SCHOOL

There were two institutions which through the years meant very much to our home and community. Without them the place would surely have been a mental and spiritual desert. They were the Danish Lutheran Church and the Danish Folk School. Both were located in the village of Nysted. This village was named for a Danish city on the island of Lolland. Nysted was founded in 1882. In the beginning, church services were held in the public school, a half mile east of Nysted. The first pastor was S. H. Madsen. He was a real pioneer soul. He could preach a sermon and build a house. In fact he built his own. He could cure the souls of men and the bodies of animals. One of my father's horses was badly cut in a barbed wire fence. Pastor Madsen was called. He asked for hot water to wash out the wound. Then he called for needle and thread, and he sewed up the wound and the horse was made whole.

The fact that these pastors from Denmark followed their people to the end of the world showed their consecration and fortitude.

When S. H. Madsen left Nysted, Pastor Skovgaard took his place. He, too, had received all of his education and training in Denmark. He was both the pastor and the headmaster of the folk school.

The first Nysted Folk School was held in a remodelled store building. The physical conditions were extremely primitive. On the opening day six students had arrived. The largest number enrolled that first winter was twelve.

One of the teachers that first winter was Mr. Peter

Ebbesen, a most interesting man. For some time he taught the local public school. Later he edited a Danish paper called **Stjernen** (The Star). He was the first Danish county treasurer. He was an authority on the history of Howard County. In 1937 I had a most interesting visit with this man. At that time he lived in California.

The first winter was an extremely cold one for the students. Pastor Skovgaard could not afford to buy coal, so the students cut green trees along Oak Creek. The exercise gave much heat, but the green wood in a stove gave little.

In the summer of 1889 Pastor Skovgaard built a new school building. It was much better than the old and put a heavy financial burden on the headmaster. The debt was not so large, but the rate of interest was. That was 24 per cent. Weary of the heavy load, Pastor Skovgaard left in 1890.

Before he left, a folk school association had been organized. The chief purpose of this was to relieve the headmaster of the financial burdens connected with the school. This organization bought the school building from Pastor Skovgaard.

Since the folk school played so large a role in the life of the Nysted community, more should be told about its early history and philosophy.

About one hundred and forty years ago, Denmark was becoming a depressed area. She had suffered much as a result of the Napoleonic Wars. Denmark had bet on the wrong horse and that horse was Napoleon. After the Battle of Waterloo in 1815, he was through.

There was one man who was deeply concerned about the plight of his people. That man was N. F. S. Grundtvig. He was a poet, a historian, a philosopher and a religious leader. He wrote songs for his people, but they did not sing them. He dreamed of a folk school, a people's school for the common man; and most of the Danes were farmers. He wanted a school that could awaken the common man to the high possibilities of life. He talked and wrote about this new school. He called it a school for life, about life. He wanted his people to be awakened to the things that are historically true, ethically noble and beautiful. All this he said should be done through the medium of the **Living Word**. The best time to do this for the young was during the ages 18-25. This is the period when youth dreams his noblest dreams.

The first folk school was founded at Rødding, Denmark. It was founded not so much to awaken the youth of Denmark as to stem the rising tide of Germanism which was pressing from the south. In 1864 Denmark lost an unequal war to Prussia and Austria. As a result of the war she also lost the duchies of Slesvig and Holstein. The Rødding school was located in Slesvig and had to be moved to Askov, north of the new boundary line.

Following the war the people of Denmark were in the deepest gloom. They had lost many of their good people and some of their best land. There was danger that Denmark would sink down and become another Albania.

The fact that this did not happen is largely due to a splendid group of young educators. They did not begin at the top. They went to the grassroots. They saw that the people must be enlightened. They knew that a truly enlightened people is not easy to whip.

One of the first successful folk schools in Denmark was founded by Kristen Kold, a great teacher, a man with deep religious convictions and with a burning zeal to help his people. His first school he helped to build with his own hands. Before the opening day came, he prayed to God that he might have at least one student. He got fifteen. His first term was for young men. He and his assistant literally lived with the students day and night. They ate at the same table and slept in the same loft. Kold said that his **aim was to wind up his students so that they would keep going for life.** He sang with the young men and talked to their hearts and minds. He had rare ability to establish mental contact with his students.

Other schools were built throughout the kingdom, and

a splendid group of young men, most of them graduates of the University of Copenhagen, went out to work among the farmers. Among the greatest of these pioneers, in addition to Kold, were Schroeder, Trier and Norregaard.

The folk school is a small school. It must be. It is a very personal school. Its leaders know that in education there can be no mass production. The teacher must love people and love learning. It was the aim of these early leaders to establish, to create an environment so charged with the good life that a young person was most likely to be influenced for life.

Often the folk schools are not co-educational. There is usually a four or five-month term for young men in winter, and a term for young women in summer. Most of the students who have attended have come from farm homes. But the folk school is not an agricultural college. It is a cultural school. The humanities have the first place.

It is true that many of the leaders have been trained for the ministry, but it is a mistake to think of the folk school as a Bible school. While there is a strong religious under-current, most often there are no courses in Bible study. The really important subjects have always been history, literature, science, song and gymnastics. Such subjects as reading, arithmetic, bookkeeping and grammar are taught, but they are of secondary importance. Furthermore, the folk school gives no credits and has no graduation. The leaders know that the really important things that happen in the human heart and mind cannot be measured and graded.

In the fall of 1891 Pastor H. C. Strandskov accepted a call to be the village pastor and the headmaster of the school. He came to Nysted from Ashland, Michigan. He, too, had come under the influence of the folk school movement in Denmark.

While he was the headmaster, a new and larger school building was erected. The older school building was remodelled into a parsonage for his growing family. Things started out well for Strandskov, but then came the serious economic depression of the 90's, and a very bad drought in 1894. These hurt the work.

It was Pastor Strandskov who started the September 8th festivals, which came to mean so much to both church and school. More will be told about these festivals later when they entered my life.

There were many meetings at the folk school, especially during the winter. The students put on plays and many people from the community came to see these and enjoyed them very much. In my childhood all the plays presented were in the Danish language. American dramatists were few and not very well known in this little Denmark. One play made a big hit, and that was Holberg's **Jeppe on the Hill**. It was the talk of town and country, and the man who took the part of Jeppe was promptly named Jeppe by the people.

Father and mother went to most of the meetings at the school. Baby sitters were unknown and we children often went with them. Before I knew who Shakespeare was I heard such names as Macbeth and Hamlet. There were many lectures by faculty members on literary and historical subjects. Quite often students and teachers had musical instruments and there was a little orchestra. While the leader was no Toscanini, it did bring some of Mozart to the prairies.

In 1886 the church was built across the road from the folk school. It was simple in design, built of wood with a high tower and spire. When one came to Nysted from the hills to the east, it was a beautiful sight with the trees along Oak Creek in the background. In a very real sense it was this church that was the center of the Nysted community life.

In my childhood we rarely missed a church service. Sunday was the best day of the week. There was better food, nicer clothes and there might be company. On a Sunday morning the church bell rang three times: one hour before the service, one-half before, and at service time. When the first bell was heard across the fields, mother would say that

29

it was time for us to leave. We were never late, and soon the horses were hitched to the buggy. As we approached the village, we could see other wagons and buggies coming toward the church. When people met in front of the tall, white church, it was evident at once that this was a holy day.

The First Nysted Church

People smiled, exchanged greetings and stood talking in small groups till the pastor came. With his arrival, all went into the sanctuary.

Inside the church was a solemn hush. To these simple people this was God's house and must not be desecrated with loud chatter. An aisle up the center divided the church into two parts. In my childhood the men sat on the right side and the women on the left. We children were divided between them.

The services were always in the Danish language. It was the only language that most of these people understood. These farmers loved to sing the old, majestic Danish hymns. Both words and music were part of the great heritage they brought with them to the New World.

The first preacher I can remember was H. C. Strandskov. He had a full beard and a most expressive face. When he

30

spoke he frequently looked upward. I was sure that he could see God and His angels in heaven.

I like to remember mother as she sat in the church pew, her large, strong hands folded as in prayer; her careworn face expressing for an hour some of the peace that passes all understanding. She often put an arm caressingly around one of us children who sat near her. At home she was so busy. Perhaps she felt she neglected to love us enough.

This is my mental picture of mother. Her hair was dark and she parted it in the middle, combed it down flat to both sides and it was drawn back into a bun. She had dark-brown eyes with dark eyelashes and eyebrows. She had rather high cheekbones and there was a sternness about her personality. When at leisure, there was a Lincolnesque sadness about her face. She, too, knew the sadness of things. She was keenly aware of change and decay in life.

I shall never forget her hands. While they were large from much hard labor, they were not awkward. There was an enormous amount of work to be done and she did it with zest. Those hands could wash dishes, sew a dress, knit a stocking, cook a meal, milk a cow, hoe a garden, box an ear and caress a sick child with equal skill.

As mentioned above, she was afraid of the prairie storms, but that fear passed with the storm. She was also much afraid of the Indians. If father was away from home and the Indians came, she was badly frightened. Once an old chief, painted up like an Easter egg, came and peered through her kitchen window and mother nearly passed out. When I saw mother's fear, I screamed!

However, mother had none of the morbidity of a Beret in **Giants in the Earth** nor the sickly longings of the farm woman in Willa Cather's **Wagner Matinee**. She was deeply thankful to God for her farm home and her children. Her wants were few and simple. She had a wonderful opportunity to forget herself in work that was everything to her. She forgot herself in something that was bigger and better than herself.

Truly mother was a remarkable woman. It is **doubtful**

31

that she had more than a fifth grade formal education, and yet she had better taste in literature than many college graduates I have known since. She never heard an opera, but she loved music deeply. She would have been ill at ease at a formal dinner table, yet there was a refinement of heart and mind that was most rare.

In religion mother was a mystic. She often talked about dreams and had strange premonitions. She had a prayer book that she used much. While she did not read the family Bible often, she did have a strong veneration for the Book. I recall a strange incident when I was about six years of age. It was early in the new year and mother was getting ready to go down into the cellar for something. As she turned to go down the steps, she happened to glance out the west window and saw the new moon. She stopped dead still and told me, with fear in her voice, to go and get the Bible. I did as told and she let it fall open and read aloud with deep pathos the first lines her eyes fell upon. I asked her why she did that and she replied that what she had read would come true within the year. I did not hear her refer to it again.

I suppose all children have some cherished memories. I hope they do. One that will always linger in my mind was when mother put us to bed. For some time she would sit quietly by us, and then we would say our evening prayers. Often with her voice filled with emotions, she told us that we must never forget that we were God's children. He would take care of us if we were good.

How she loved her simple, prairie home! We never drove away from the place for any length of time but that she would look back at the house and say, "Then in God's name."

V

LIFE ON THE FARM

Shortly after the twins were born, an addition was built to our house. That gave us three bedrooms and a parlor. This room was different. When I first remember it, there was wall-to-wall carpeting. While this was surely not oriental, it was nice and not very common in the country. The parlor was used only on special occasions such as the larger birthday parties or when some people of greater importance came. The most important family among us was the preacher's.

Of course, mother did all the work about the house; though all of us, as soon as we could, did lighter tasks. Mother milked the cows until the older children were strong enough to do that. I never saw my father milk a cow. Men in Europe did not do that. During the busy season, mother also helped with some field work. She knew how to pitch hay and pick corn.

For some years after mother came to her farm home, she washed the family washing on a washboard. This contraption contained a sheet of corrugated metal set in a wooden frame. The frame was put down diagonally into a tub of sudsy, hot water with the top of the frame leaning against the side of the tub. Here mother stood and rubbed the wet clothes vigorously on the corrugated metal. She stood in a stooped position and I can imagine that it was tiring.

In our day I know that the washboard would be considered an instrument of torture. But for ages the women washed the family washing in a brook or river, and most often without the help of soap. I saw this method in 1953 in both France and Italy.

When she saw that the clothes were clean, she would take them out of the water. White clothes were then boiled on the kitchen stove. This was not a gas or an electric stove. Wood was scarce and we burned what we could find; corn cobs, sticks and cow chips. Father could have been more considerate in this matter of fuel supply. He left that largely to mother and us children.

When the dark clothes had been washed, she wrung them out by hand. She did the same with the white clothes when they had been boiled thoroughly. The clothes were then hung on an outside clothes line. In cold winter weather, the clothes froze dry. In summer they dried quickly, but dust storms were an enemy of clean clothes. This method of cleaning clothes was so difficult and precarious that clothes often were worn a long time before being cleaned again.

We had no running water in our house. Of course, we had no indoor toilet. Such a thing would surely have been considered both indecent and filthy. We had no bathtub and no bathroom. In summer we had our baths in the old swimming hole or the stock tank, and in winter there was a tub bath, in the living room for nine people, and a very special occasion that was. Mother worked hard to keep us and the house clean, and that was not easy in a dust-filled country. How mother winced when an uncouth farmer spat on her clean floor!

Practically all of our food was prepared at home. The only tin can food I recall in the mid-nineties was an occasional can of salmon and sardines. Mother made cheese, butter, cured meat, baked bread and did the canning when fruit was to be had. For some time mother sent butter to some friends in Wyoming. We had a churn, a barrel-shaped thing, which we turned round and round. As soon as I was old enough, it was my job to churn butter. I was completely convinced that our churn was the poorest in the United States. When mother was not keeping an eye on me, I

34

frequently gave it the works by spinning it around at high speed. That operation, however, did not seem to speed the coming of the butter. But how good the buttermilk tasted when I had finished the task! After each churning, we had buttermilk soup for dinner. I loved it.

However, it seemed that I was always hungry, especially for fruit and sweets. In the hard times of 1894, there was talk in our home of allowing each child so many slices of bread for each meal. In those days bread had not been turned into cotton, and it was the staff of life. The rationing was tried out, but the plan was abandoned when the clamor for food became too great.

My father visited Denmark in 1893 and when he returned home we children had our first taste of bananas. Once I was with father to St. Paul, our county seat town, and I recall vividly that he gave me some dates. When father had been in town, he nearly always brought some sweets home for his hungry children. When we saw him coming down the road, two or three of us would run to meet him. One day he came from town and I alone ran to meet him. I asked if he had anything for me and he said that he did not, but I was certain that he was fooling me. When he left the wagon, I ransacked a box which contained some packages. I found a small paper package, securely tied up. I could not get it open with my fingers, so I bit a hole in the paper with my teeth. Since I did not like the taste of the powder, I put it down. When I came into the house, mother noticed that my lips were covered with a green color, and she inquired of father. In alarm they gave me all the antidotes they could think of, but the rat poison had no effect on me. I don't know if it did on the rats.

It is true that we children were nearly always hungry, but we did not starve. It must be remembered, however, that there was a severe depression in the nineties and that there were frequent crop failures on the prairies. Times were hard and I can member that father and J. C. Jensen talked about moving.

During difficult years mother showed much ingenuity

in feeding her big family. We were seven or eight children and the good times did not come in Nebraska till early in the present century. Modern children would be astonished to see some of our meals. They would pity or despise us. For many an evening meal, after a long and hard day, we had milk and bread for supper. Mother put some little pieces of white and dark bread into a large bowl of skimmed milk. With this we ate bread with a lard spread. We sold our butter. On the lard we put a little salt. I liked sugar on my lard.

Before we bought the cream separator, this milk was hand-skimmed and was fairly rich. Our bread must not be confused with modern bakery bread. Our white bread was not highly refined and bleached. Our rye bread was always made from whole flour and mother was an excellent baker. It was a sin to throw away the least bit of bread.

Mother was an inventor of many dishes. It was porridge, porridge, and we liked it. People were expected to eat what was set before them on the table. Mother made these porridges: rice, corn meal, starch, oat meal, rhubarb, currant, gooseberry and apple. Naturally, some of these things we did not have all the time but when things were in season, mother used them. Often there were wild plums, choke cherries, gooseberries and grapes along Oak Creek, and we children helped our parents pick them.

Mother was also good at making gruels of such things as rice, sago and buttermilk. Then there were soups. I recall these: chicken, cabbage, kale, beef, pork, split pea, bean and bread soup.

On our farm we always had chickens, ducks and pigeons. These gave us fresh meat from time to time throughout the year. Here, however, there was a conflict of interests. Mother took care of the poultry and what money she made from the sale of eggs, she used for the household. If all the chickens were eaten, there would be no eggs to sell.

My brother, Anker, was an enthusiastic hunter, and I trudged behind him many, many miles when he was hunting for rabbit and prairie chicken. Any game that we brought home was most welcome.

Father and mother liked fish very much. In the Scandinavian countries fish has long been an important part of the poor man's diet. But father was not much impressed with Nebraska sea food! Often when he was in town, he would try to buy good fish from the local butcher; and if he succeeded, we all celebrated.

As mentioned above, we cured our own meat. Hams and bacon slabs were put into brine and later smoked. Early, it was my job to take care of the smoking of meat. I don't know who invented our smoking establishment, but whoever did should be told that it was greatly in need of improvement. This is how father told me to make it, and I set to work with the help of my younger brother, Holger. We found a barrel, made a hole in the one side near the bottom and put it into the ground so this hole opened into a tunnel that connected the barrel with a fire pit. When this was accomplished, we hung hams and slabs of bacon in the barrel and covered the top with a wire screen. We then found some kindling and built a fire. Mother or father usually supervised this act, since we were never allowed to use matches without supervision. The danger of fire was great. If the wind was in the right direction, the barrel was soon filled with smoke, and the meat was being smoked to a delicacy. But when our smoking establishment did not have a tail wind, our good meat hung there lonely and neglected. I always suspected that the whole idea was father's and I complained to him that it would not work, but he was above the "war clouds" and told me to try again. It would work if we did things right. Holger and I scoured the place for combustible and "smokible" materials, but we had very little success till the wind changed. It took time to cure meat. Our patience wore thin and we played hookey. It was not nearly so interesting to smoke meat as it was to make a threshing machine or a wagon. But mother kept after us and in one way or the other we got the meat smoked and it was carefully buried under the oats in the oats bin.

We always raised our own potatoes and we used many of them. We nearly always had potatoes for one meal a day. Fat bacon we ate nearly every day. When there was no material for brown gravy, mother made a milk gravy. This was not as good as brown gravy, but it was better than nothing.

During the heavy work of the harvest season, mother made a light beer. We all consumed much of this, and it seemed to quench thirst much better than water.

All during the year, we ate a light lunch in the middle of the forenoon and again in the middle of the afternoon.

Where there were so many children going to school at the same time, it took many sandwiches. There were, of course, no hot lunches in school. There was a time when six of us trudged off to school in the morning. As mentioned elsewhere, mother usually used a lard as spread on our bread. On this she might sprinkle some salt or sugar. Molasses was used as was also cheese and meat.

The Danes are supposed to be an imaginative people. The world's best fairy tale writer, Hans Christian Andersen, was a Dane. Strange is it not that Danish surnames show so little evidence of imagination. In the Nysted community there were Jensens, Christensens, Nielsens, Larsens, Hansens, Hermansens et al. However, when it came to giving nicknames there was evidence of imagination. Here are a few: Fandemand (Satan's man), Rød Jørn (Red Jorgen), Gal Petersen (Mad Petersen), Hans Lutter Løgn (Hans All Lies), Kong Niels (King Niels) and Nummer Een (Number One).

There were some interesting characters among the Danish immigrants.

Any man who has encountered a walking plow that refuses to scour, knows how exasperating that is, and will have a deep feeling of kinship with an unhappy Dane who was trying to plow a field with rich, heavy clay. Of course, the plow refused to scour. He spoke to it tenderly and with no cooperation. He cursed it and to no avail. This called for action. He left the horses and the plow in the field,

38

ran to the house, about forty rods away, took his old, trusted musket, loaded it carefully, ran back to the stubborn plow and shot it. There is nothing recorded on how many times he shot it, or if it scoured beautifully after the burst of the old musket and the farmer's temper. It is said that he felt better afterwards. Perhaps it was worth the effort.

There was another farmer whose heart was as big as a pumpkin. He loved his wife dearly. In the course of their married life, the poor woman gradually took on more and more weight. Finally she was so heavy that it was nearly impossible to get her into the farm wagon. But this kind Dane was a resourceful man. He learned that he could load her into the wagon if she would first climb upon a low platform. However, it was not convenient to carry a platform about the country. What did the clever Dane do? He got down on all four and let big mama step up on him, and from his strong back into the wagon. The problem was solved.

Central Nebraska is a windy country. It is a good place for windmills. They really do their work. There was one serious drawback about the windmill and that was that the thing needed lubricating oil from time to time. In a windy country this could be a dangerous undertaking. One courageous Dane answered the cry of his windmill on a windy day. He applied oil copiously to the dry bearings, but just at that moment a heavy gust of wind blew across the plains, the farmer lost his grip and fell — fell right through the roof of his milk house. The story goes that he fell into the milk tank. However, there is no proof of this, but it is true that this Viking suffered no ill effects from the great fall.

One local character had earned a considerable reputation as a veterinarian. Now he was not a graduate of any leading university, but he loved all the dumb creatures. From time to time he was called to a farm to save a sick animal. Once he came to a farm where a pig was very ill. He diagnosed the case carefully and the verdict was: appendicitis. He performed immediate surgery. He pronounced the operation a success. But alas, the pig was dead!

Another farmer had a sick horse. He called the same horse doctor. He came, examined the animal carefully, and told the farmer to bring a lighted, farm lantern. The farmer brought the lantern and he was told to go to the rear of the sick horse lift the tail and hold the lantern near the anus. The doctor now opened the horse's mouth and looked into it and after a moment exclaimed, "Your horse has a strangulated gut!" What he did to the horse is not known, but it is claimed that the animal lived to a ripe old age.

As mentioned earlier three of mother's brothers tried life in America. Only one remained here till his death and that was Mathias. The one we knew best was Uncle Jorgen. He had large, strong hands and a very bald head. He was a kind-hearted soul and was considered a bit queer among practical people. It is doubtful that he ever felt quite at home in the United States. He never was able to find a girl in this country who would marry him. Perhaps he was not able to find a girl that he really cared for. He became a bachelor. Eventually he tired of bachelorhood and left for Denmark where he found a wife. They both came to America and we children loved both of them. She was an excellent housekeeper.

Since neither was young and no children came, they decided to adopt a boy. Uncle took a train to Omaha and visited an orphanage to look for a boy. Imagine the consternation in that little Denmark in Howard County when he returned home with a little, cute Chinese boy of five whose name was Willie Dikahota. He had dark, straight hair, yellowish skin, high cheekbones and slanting eyes. Among the many, towheaded children of the Nysted community, he looked as much out of place as an ugly duckling among stately swans. All of their friends were dumbfounded and asked why in creation he did not get a Danish boy or at least a child who looked like one. Unhappy Uncle Jorgen replied that Willie was the only boy he could get, and that they had him on trial.

For some weeks they kept him and this Oriental child

began to learn the Danish tongue. But perhaps they felt in appearance there was too much difference between Willie and the other children in the community. At any rate, before the trial period had expired, Jorgen took the boy by train back to Omaha.

A day or two later Uncle Jorgen returned from Omaha and with him again was Willie Dikahota. Great was the surprise of all good Danes. When asked why he did not leave the boy in Omaha, he replied that he did not have the heart. Willie had cried so hard when he left that he regretted the act and had decided to keep the boy. He was now legally adopted.

Soon Willie was in public school and soon he spoke both the American and the Danish languages. If he had ever known the Chinese language, it was forgotten.

Uncle Jorgen and his wife were perhaps too old to know how to bring up this strange child. He soon learned that he could get his way if he cried hard enough. If either or both of them occasionally became firm and insisted upon obedience, Willie would go into an awful tantrum and then he got his way. As time went on he became more and more incorrigible. It was surely little joy they had from him.

One year Uncle Jorgen was not well and decided to go to a clinic in Omaha for a check-up. He took Willie with him. Perhaps he was afraid that his wife would not be able to handle him. On the train Jorgen fell asleep and when he woke up, his wallet was gone. It was commonly believed that Willie had stolen it.

The lad ran away and many years later my brother, Holger, saw him in Yankton, South Dakota. He was with a medicine show and stood outside a tent barking his wares. He had a good voice.

It did not seem possible for Uncle and Aunt to feel at home in America. For a while they tried Denmark and found that they were strangers there too. They came back and lived in Dannebrog for a few years. Here too they were homeless. Their last move was to Denmark where both are buried. As long as they lived, Willie continued to hound them for money and told the most fantastic stories about his ill fortune. After their passing, he was killed in an automobile wreck.

Among the Danes who lived in our neighborhood, none was influenced less by America than Kristen Moller and his family. They remained Danish to the last. It seemed that Mrs. Moller sewed all the clothes for the family, and in the most unusual shapes and styles. In a community with many odd people, I looked at Mr. Moller' trousers with astonishment. They were buttoned across his spacious stomach with large buttons, and the whole front when unbuttoned fell down and was parallel with Mother Earth. Mr. Moller was a sociable soul and liked to visit with his neighbors, but his thrifty wife kept an eagle eye on him, and when she thought he had talked long enough, she would come out of the house and give him the signal that talking time was up. He would go back to his work with a grumble. At times he cursed his fate, but not his wife.

While the Mollers were indifferent to fashions in clothes, they were progressive in mechanical things. They had one of the first internal combustion engines I saw. They used its power to grind feed for their stock. It was on this farm that I saw my first cream separator. I was with my parents there one evening while the chores were being done, and I saw Mr. Moller use the machine. He gave me a cup of fresh, warm, skim milk. To my mind this was much better than hand-skimmed milk. I noticed that father was very much interested in this machine and asked many questions about it. It is interesting and somewhat unusual that the Mollers could not get used to America. They had a big farm sale and went back to Denmark, never to return.

One day father came from Dannebrog and told us with an air of authority that he was interested in buying a cream separator. He told us that this machine was widely used by the more progressive farmers of Denmark, and that the

42

machine method of skimming milk was more efficient than the old hand method. We boys were interested at once, but mother objected. She felt that the buying of the machine was a criticism of her method of skimming milk, and that it would mean more work for her to keep it clean. She knew from Mrs. Moller that that was no easy task. However, father was not a man to be side-tracked from a new idea. He persisted and one day came home with a brand new Sharples cream separator.

It was set up in the milk house. It was about as inconvenient as American inventive genius could make a machine. But father was proud of it. It was very high and had no legs to stand on. While father was no good as a mechanic, he did manage to build a platform for it. However, the container into which we must pour the milk was way up there. Father made a platform we could stand on when pouring the milk into the container, but to get onto the platform required real dexterity. The one who turned the machine was in danger of being doused with fresh, warm milk. We did not like a milk shower, but father told us that a little milk would not hurt anybody.

That machine was the most tempermental thing made by man. Without the slightest provocation it would begin to vibrate. In the beginning it fillled us with fear and trembling. The very milk house was shaken to its foundation, but father insisted that such was the price of progress.

Mother's objection to the thing was well founded. It was hard to keep clean. It had a thing called a bowl. This was heavy, complicated and filled with secret caverns. To keep it clean was beyond the power of ordinary mortals. There were tubes in it that became clogged and then all scientific principles went awry. Often mother had to go back to the hand method again. She told father that she did not like the thing. It was a burden. However, it stayed there, and I suppose farm women have been wrestling with them ever since.

As far as I can remember, mother had a good vegetable garden, if drouth and the grasshoppers did not get it before she did. She always had some flowers and cared for them tenderly.

There was little serious illness among us children. There was no talk of vitamins and calories. Like other children we had our fair share of measles, mumps, toothache, earache, colds and other ailments that children seem to get whether they live in the country or the city. It was always mother who took care of us. There must have been times when she went without sleep for days. One winter my sister, Agneta, and my baby brother, Holger, contracted the smallpox. He was very ill. His little body was covered with boils, and mother cared for him day and night. She nursed him so well that he recoverd completely.

In addition to all the other tasks, mother did the sewing for the family. Father was the only one whose work clothes were bought at the store. In some way she managed to keep clothes on our backs. She sewed all my clothes except my underwear. Until I was about twelve, mother sewed blue jeans for all of us boys. I recall vividly that some of the other boys had jeans that were bought in the store. These seem so much nicer as they had many pockets. I begged mother for more pockets too. She became impatient and scolded me. However, the next pair of jeans she made for me had a surprise. They had one right hip pocket, but none in front. I groaned in mortal agony. I protested so strongly that it nearly brought mother to tears.

She sewed pants, shirts, and coats for us boys; and skirts, dresses, and nightgowns for the girls. We boys had not become worldly enough to wear nightshirts. We slept in our underwear in winter and in our shirts in summer. In addition to all this sewing, mother knitted stockings and mittens for us. I can see her as she sat by the light of the old kerosene lamp, the needles going so fast that the eyes could hardly follow them.

Knitting required yarn and yarn cost money. Since money was scarce, mother spun most of the yarn. We children helped her card wool. When we had made high piles of the fluffy, woolen rolls, mother would sit down to the spinning

44

wheel and make the yarn. I liked to watch when she did that, and more than once I had my fingers slapped for interfering with that wonderful machine.

The reader may wonder how my parents managed to live in a rather small house with so many children. It was order or chaos and my parents chose order. But my parents knew that children do not fall in love with a switch. They wanted to give us something worthwhile and something lasting. To this end they read hundreds of stories to us.

In the winter evenings when the chores were finished and the supper dishes done, father would bring out a novel and mother would get her knitting. He read remarkably well. The books were in the Danish and of the romantic kind. Most of the books were so interesting that we begged father to read on and on. There were times when he kept reading till eleven o'clock. Maybe all this was not good for our bodies, but it was a wonderful thing for our souls.

When we had been up late for our reading, it was hard to get up in the morning, and to get all the chores done before school. Mother was usually up first and that was about 6:45. The house could be terribly cold and she got dressed as fast as possible, lit two or three kerosene lamps and went to the kitchen to start a fire in the kitchen stove. In the evening it was my task to find some dry straw and some kindling so that she could start the fire quickly. She then started a fire in the living room stove and called the family. We children were as dead and it took threats and kind words to get us out of a warm bed. Our bedroom was arctic and it did not take us long to get dressed and be downstairs. Mother told us how much time we had in which to do the chores, eat breakfast and to reach school before nine o'clock. Usually Anker took care of the horses and the horse barn, while Chris, one of the girls and I did the milking. We rushed off to the milk house, got the milk pails and into the warm barn. First we fed the cows. In winter we generally milked ten or twelve cows. We milked those cows and fed the cats warm milk. When this was done, father took care of the milk. Before that he had slopped the pigs and had fed the feed steers. Chris and I cleaned the cow barn.

In the meantime, mother and the girls had been busy in the house. One of the first tasks was to bring in fresh water. They filled the stove reservoir and the water pail in the kitchen. By eight o'clock we had finished our part of the chores and were in the house to clean up for school. Our breakfast was rather light. We did not have pancakes for that meal. In Denmark they have those for lunch or supper and mother followed that custom. We had oatmeal, milk and bread. During most of my childhood, we did not use much butter for our bread. Mother sold that. After breakfast we set out for school. The mile walk against a cold wind was good exercise. Calories were not a problem.

It was something of a problem to get books. Fortunately there was a library at the folk school and the pastor also had a library. Only once did father go modern in his selection of books. He tried one of Tolstoy's. That was too deep for us. We protested, not because it was Russian, but because we did not find it interesting. It is incredible the number of good stories that our parents read to us during those years.

The presence of books and the reading of them, gave our barnyard a literary aroma. We children named each new calf for some character in fiction. If a newborn heifer was especially beautiful, she would be given the name of some highborn and lovely maid from literature. A fine bull calf was similarly honored. If a scrub calf made its appearance, it was named for the villain of a book. If names from literature were not available, we resorted to history. When a heifer showed early signs of being voluptuous, we named her Cleopatra. Like her namesake, this lusty creature came to an untimely end.

Our love for the farm animals was sincere and our naming of calves and colts was a simple manifestation of this. Much of our play was with pets. To teach a gentle calf to drink was fun, but anybody who could teach an obstreperous calf to drink without losing his temper should be given the

Congressional Medal of Honor. We often had some colts and to break them was a thrill.

We had a bay mare who was the pet of the family. She was a lady of charm, and a natural aristocrat among horses. Just to see her run was proof of that. One day father told us that the mare, named Molly, was not well. We cared for her the best we knew, but she got worse. Father called Jens Andersen, the midwife's husband, who was reputed to be something of a veterinarian. He came. He bled her. We stood with bated breath while this was being done. In a few hours she died. All of us children were in tears.

But all was not fun and joy with the farm animals. We had our trials too. One day I lost control of a horse I was riding and it ran home at full speed with me clinging to it for dear life. Into the barn it ran and my head hit a beam. I fell off. Except for a bump on my head, I suffered no damage.

One day my brother, Chris, and I were driving along a country road in a cart with a frisky horse pulling us. Suddenly a dog appeared in the road. The horse reared, spun around and off it went with us clinging to the cart. It ran through a barbed wire fence, broke the harness and was off. There was the cart, straddling a wire fence, with Chris and me on each side of the wire and not badly hurt.

Once we bought a bull calf and father and Chris went to fetch it. They loaded it into a wagon and set out for home. On the way they crossed a pasture and father gave the reins to Chris while he opened a gate. The team became frightened and ran at full speed across the prairies. When they crossed some deep ruts, the wagon reach broke and Chris, bull and wagon box flew up into the air and dropped to the ground upside down. Father ran as fast as he could toward the wreckage and as he came to the wagon box, Chris came crawling out from under it and cried, "Father, I could not hold those crazy horses." In the meantime the frightened horses were running about with the two front wheels of the wagon. A farmer finally caught them.

One blot on my happy childhood was cows. For some

years I chased them during the day and they pursued me at night in my dreams. When my two older brothers began to help with field work, it was my responsibility to look after these creatures. I might be in the middle of some absorbing, childish construction project, and my mother or one of my sisters would yell, "The cows are in the corn. Go and get them right away." Here I was building a bridge or making a wonderful threshing machine and I had to leave that to chase cows! There was no justice. I ran through the tall corn to find them. I cried. I called them all the bad names I dared to use. How I wished that cows had not been included in Noah's Ark. To this day, I wish that electric fences had been invented then. Had that been true, I would gladly have electrocuted the whole herd of cows.

At this time father bought a piece of land about a mile from home. It was my misfortune that there was a cow pasture on this farm. During the summer months it was my job to drive the cows to pasture in the morning and to go for them in the evening. I always walked.

One day when I was about eight, lightning struck not far from the cows and me. The crash of thunder filled the cows with fear and me with terror. I became deathly afraid of lightning and thunder. It was plainly a phobia. All day long I would scan the skies to see if a black cloud were appearing. If there was I begged to be allowed to fetch the cows right away. I cried and my elders laughed at me, but to me this was no laughing matter. In all my life I have not been so afraid of anything as I was of thunderstorms at that time. But mother and father were not of the kind to give way to a child's silly whim. I drove the cows to pasture in spite of lightning, thunder and evil spirits.

However, our parents were usually not cruel to us. In a day when corporal punishment was most common, I do not remember that any of us children received a whipping. I never saw father slap any of us children. He simply told us what to do and we did it. Naturally, we did not do all these tasks with enthusiasm, but we did them without a murmur — if father were near.

A large family has its advantages. Kids learn to take it. The youngster who can't is made the object of ridicule. He has to be a good sport or live the life of a temporary outcast. We worked in groups. Three of us usually did the milking. I know that the cows were not milked scientifically, and I can imagine that we broke all the rules of animal husbandry. We squirted fresh milk at each other. We taught cats, dogs and even pigs to catch a stream of warm milk straight from a cow's teat. We quarreled and fought one moment about who should milk a certain cow, and laughed uproariously the next when a calf went on a rampage.

I loved the company of my brothers, sisters and other children from the neighborhood. I did not like to be alone, but I did spend much time by myself in the summer. When harvesting was done, I herded the cattle on the stubble fields to keep them out of the corn. At that time I did not have a pony. I chased the cows on foot. The sharp stubbles and thistles hurt my feet. In summer all children went barefooted. Shoes cost money.

There I was alone with the cows! I longed for the wide, wide world. On quiet days I could hear the whistle of a train going to Boelus and of a train going to Grand Island. I loved trains. I dreamed of the time when I could see strange lands and fine people. I told myself a thousand times that when I grew up I would see the sights of the world and be among the great. When I happened to be in Dannebrog with my parents and heard that a train was coming in, I asked them if I might go and see the train. They usually let me go. I stood there pop-eyed, looking with envy at those important and happy trainmen. The fact is, that like most rural children of that day, I was very timid in the presence of town folks.

One man I always saw at the railway depot was little Mauritz Andersen. He was an odd and interesting person. He wore wooden shoes and in a hand cart carried the outgoing mail to the trains and the incoming mail to the post office. He did this for decades. He was also the village shoemaker and was conscientious about his work, and his prices were low. He was a deeply religious man and when someone called at his tiny shop, he was often given a little sermon free. He was worried about the sins of his fellow men, and if smoking a pipe and drinking a glass of beer would keep a man from entering heaven, he had good reasons for worrying. It seemed that most of the men did that. This was one of his: "If God had wanted you to smoke tobacco, He would have created you with a chimney, would He not?" The skeptics found it difficult to answer that one.

One of my early adventures was to drive with father when he hauled grain to the mill to have it ground into flour. We usually drove to St. Paul where there was a flour mill. It took all day. The trip to the village must have taken at least three hours, but the time did not seem long. Father had been impatient to be off, but once on the way, his pipe lighted, he was in good spirits. Then he began to tell me stories of his experiences in the homeland. How I liked to listen to his pleasant voice!

When we had reached St. Paul we drove to the mill, unloaded the grain and gave the horses a rest and feed in the livery barn. Here we ate our sandwiches. We usually went up town. This was the largest town I had seen and I thought it most thrilling. If the harvest had been good, father might go on a spending spree. He allowed himself a glass of beer and me a bottle of pop. What luxury! Later in the day, we drove back to the mill and picked up the flour. We always bought enough in the fall to last us through the winter.

Only once was I outside the county till I was seventeen years of age. I was not on a train till that time. I must have been about six when my parents and a neighboring couple decided to visit some friends near Central City, about fifty miles away. For some reason they decided to take me along. We drove in our open buggy and our neighbor furnished the horses. I don't remember much about the trip, but I do remember that we had driven about twelve miles and were in the sand hills to the east of Dannebrog when the bright sun arose. It was a brilliant summer morning.

At Central City the horses were watered and given a feed. We ate the lunch, which the ladies had prepared, in the shade of a tree. No one thought of going to a cafe for lunch.

It is strange what one remembers from childhood. I remember the long wooden bridge across the Platte River. I also remember that the people we visited had many flies and that they had good corn. It had been too dry for ours.

But I was not always the lucky one. Once in my childhood a circus came to St. Paul. How I learned about it was that some men came to Nysted and covered one of the church barns with pictures telling about this world of wonders. We children were absorbed with these pictures. Never had we seen anything like them. There were pictures of animals that we had never seen: lions, tigers, elephants, giraffes and horrible snakes. There were funny looking clowns, and young men and women on the flying trapeze. We children spent hours looking at these pictures.

I told my parents about them. I knew from past experience that it would take great effort to wear down their outstanding ability to resist. I kept at it, and my brothers and sisters joined me in this noble effort. We used all manner of subtle suggestions and hints about going to the circus. It was father who began to weaken and my joy was unbounded. But I was riding for a hard fall. One evening he announced, with an air of finality, that he and the four older children would drive to St. Paul to see the circus. I would have to stay home and help mother with the chores. Then he announced my consolation prize: I could go with mother that day to Ladies' Aid. I went through an inferno, but tears and supplications were of no help.

The day came. They, with many others in our community, drove to the circus. I drove with mother to

Ladies' Aid. Part of the way she let me drive the horse. That made me feel big.

Father wanted his children to be well informed. One day he came from town carrying a large map of the United States. It had been put out by the Burlington Railway and father was proud of it. He evidently thought that our knowledge of our country's map was imperfect. It was. He set out to correct this defect. He hung it on the living room wall, behind the stove. Mother objected. She did not think it was a thing of beauty. Father overruled her objections and told her that our future demanded it. Perhaps it did. The map was fun.

In the evening when father was not reading to us, he liked to pretend that he was a schoolmaster. He sent one of us to the map and told him to locate a river. When one failed, he would send another to the map. He would name a state and ask the child at the map to locate it and ask what the capital was. One by one we went to the map, and little by little we learned many things about it.

At an early age I made up my mind that farming was not an exciting occupation. I would not be a farmer when I grew up. The only other occupation I had a chance to see in our immediate community was that of a blacksmith. While he did not have a spreading chestnut tree, I did think that would be the life for me. My interest began to wane when I saw our local smith try to shoe a hostile horse. Maybe that was exciting, but it was also very hard and very dangerous. The blacksmith was both tired and angry. When the job was finally finished, I noticed that he was wringing wet with sweat.

My next ambition was far higher. It happened that I went with father to the railway station in Dannebrog and saw the agent send a telegram. He did it with dignity and dispatch. Now there was something for a rising young fellow! I am sure I dreamed about being a telegrapher most of the way home.

For some time I had been answering advertisements

in our weekly papers. In reply I had received nothing but a few circulars. Then one day I saw an advertisement in a paper about York College, and my heart skipped a beat when I saw that they taught the occupation of my best dreams: telegraphy. I wrote a letter to the college in my best handwriting. I had not yet mastered the Spencerian method of penmanship. A few days later I received a catalogue from the college. I was disappointed. It looked so drab. I feared it was a lost cause.

Some weeks later Chris and I were working in a field. I was small, barefooted and in homemade jeans. I certainly did not look like a fine station agent. Suddenly I saw a man coming across the field toward me. He was tall, wore a dark suit, a white shirt and tie, and a white straw hat. I stopped my work, screwed up my courage in preparation to meet this distinguished looking man. He gave me a condescending look and asked me if I was Alfred Nielsen. I was. Well, he represented York College, and asked if I was still interested in telegraphy. I told him that I was indeed. Then he said, "When you get old enough to go to college, I hope you will consider York College." With that he left me. He had taken a train from York to Dannebrog, hired a team at the livery barn to see a bashful boy. I never attended York College.

However, my interest in telegraphy did not die at once. I earned enough money to buy a telegraph set with a book of instructions on how to become a telegraph operator. Our house for some time was filled with the spirit of Samuel Morse, the clicking of the telegraph, and secret messages.

VI

HOLIDAYS

Christmas was the most important holiday of the year and also the longest vacation. We lived in great anticipation of it. Long before the holidays, mother began to make things for it. We usually butchered a pig before Christmas. This animal was usually a large one that had had special care. The day for butchering had to be a cold one so the carcass could be chilled. One of the first jobs was to sharpen the knives. We had an old grindstone back of the shed and while one of us turned the grindstone, father would sharpen the knives. In the meantime, mother was heating a boiler full of water for the ordeal.

We roped the pig and led him to the place of execution. He was tied and then stuck, amidst the most dreadful squeals, till the main artery was severed. There was now a fountain of blood, and one of us held a bucket to catch it. Soon the squeal ceased and the pig was dead. Now the boiling water was put into a barrel and the pig was scalded. Once that was done, it was placed on a table for scraping. Each of us took a knife to remove the hair. I don't know how much good we did, but we did our best and father was usually patient with us. When the pig had been scraped and washed, it was hung up by its hind legs and the cutting began. Intestines, stomach, lungs, bladder, kidneys and other organs were removed, and the operation was soon complete.

Now there were good things to eat. Out of the blood mother made blood sausage. We liked it. The intestines were cleaned for sausage casings. All of the liver, kidneys and tongue were used. One interesting custom of our neighborhood was that when one had butchered, he would bring fresh meat to some of the other neighbors. When another butchered, he would return the favor. In an age when there was no refrigeration, it gave us fresh meat oftener.

Before we came to Christmas, the larder was usually quite full. The evening of December 23rd was called Little Christmas Eve, and it was for the animals. The horses, the cattle, the pigs, the cats and even the sparrows were given extra food. They, too, must know that Christ was born.

Some time before the holidays a topic of discussion among us children was whether or not we would have a Christmas tree. We would ask father and mother and the reply was often that we could not afford it. We never saw the tree till Christmas Eve.

On that day we had been very busy. We had tried to get so much work done that there would be as little as possible to do during the holidays, which lasted from December 24 till January 3. Again Christmas Eve the animals were treated better than usual. We had to be through with our evening chores by sunset. At that time the Christmas chimes would peal from the Nysted church. At sunset father, mother and we children would wait outside, facing the west, and stand there waiting reverently for the chimes. How beautiful they sounded. They lasted for about five minutes and during that time we were silent. Mother was always stirred by this experience. When the chimes had ceased, we wished each other Happy Christmas in the Danish language.

For many years our nearest neighbors, J. C. Jensens, came to our house for Christmas Eve, or we were at their home. We lived about a half mile apart and were the best of friends. There were many children, and what a table mother and the girls had set. In the late nineties we were eighteen souls at this festive table. After singing grace, our parents filled a small glass with wine. With many a Skoal, Skoal, and best wishes for a good Christmas, they lifted their glasses and drank in high spirits. It was a puzzle to us children that our parents could sit and eat so calmly and slowly. Had they no imagination? Somewhere in the house stood the Christmas tree loaded with presents. If the meal took too long, we asked our parents to hurry a bit.

When the meal was finally finished, father and J. C. Jensen settled down for a good after dinner smoke. If times were fairly good, they smoked a cigar. The aroma of the cigars was a sure indication that it was Christmas.

While the men were smoking, mother, Mrs. Mary Jensen and the girls did the dishes. To me it seemed that this took forever. I urged them to hurry.

As mentioned before, we children were never certain that we would have a Christmas tree. We were never allowed to see it before Christmas Eve. It was the deepest secret. In the hard years of the early nineties, there were times when my parents felt that they could not afford to buy an evergreen. Such a tree cost twenty-five cents and they did not have much money. Father would then go down to Oak Creek and find a suitable size elm tree. It is amazing what loving hands can do to put the spirit of Christmas into a naked elm tree. It seemed that we children were as happy when we danced around a poor elm tree as when we danced around a proud fir.

At last mother and Mary Jensen, very quietly, went into the nearly sacred parlor, and we children lined up in front of the closed door, and waited and waited. How father and J. C. could sit and talk in this hour of glory so indifferently about mundane affairs seemed sacrilegious. At last the door was opened. Yes, there was a tree! There it stood and never were burning candles so bright! How we had waited for this moment. It was all too good to be true.

We children were told to sit down on the floor, and father took the family Bible and read the old and ever new story: **Now it came to pass in those days, that there went out a decree from Caesar Augustus**...... While he read, we children listened — halfway. There under the tree were the presents, neatly wrapped, and how we longed for some new playthings.

When the Christmas story had been read, mother brought

the Danish hymnals and we all joined in the singing. Following that we formed a large circle and danced around the tree. A favorite song for this was, **Nu har Vi Jul Igen.** In translation it means, **Now we have Christmas again.** This was fun and we became very noisy in doing the dance. Our elders watched the candles. The presents must be distributed before these burned down. Mother and Mary Jensen distributed the gifts. They were small and most often mother had made them. It could be a pair of mittens, a pair of stockings or a woolen scarf. We had hoped for so much and received so little. For a moment the disappointment was real. But the sorrows of childhood, while intense, do not last long.

It must be very difficult for the children of our times to understand how little the pioneer children had in the way of things. Our parents were either too poor or too frugal to buy them. As far back as I can remember I wanted a wagon to play with. I begged for it year in and year out. Each year I was so sure that a wagon would be my Christmas present. But I never did get one. While this hurt me at the time, perhaps it was not so bad. I made my own wagon, and it could run as fast as any bought in a store.

When the candles on the tree had burned low and had been put out, we settled down for the evening. The Jensens and my parents enjoyed each other so much that it was often eleven o'clock by the time the party broke up. In the meantime, some of the younger children were lying on the floor fast asleep. When the time came to go home, it was quite a chore to wake them up. We nearly always walked to our nearest neighbors. The smallest children were carried. The older children walked, helping the younger.

We did things as families. The young were not uneasy in the company of adults. They worked and played together. How we loved to listen to the conversation of our elders.

Christmas day was of course an important church holiday. On that day more people attended church than usual. The church service was pretty much as other Sundays, except on that day the pastor was given a special offering and this was laid on the altar. Our whole family attended this service. My parents were very active in the church. My father must have been president of the congregation for at least twenty years. In a very real sense, the church was the center of our lives. It was from there we received so much guidance and inspiration.

There was also a church service on second Christmas day, that is December 26. This was not attended so well as the one on Christmas day.

During the holidays there was, of course, much visiting. Since there was no school, we children had much time for play and visiting.

On New Year's Eve, there was again a celebration. During early pioneer times, parties of men walked or drove throughout the community, went up to a farm house and fired shots. The guns were heavily loaded and the blasts were terrific. When the men had fired their guns, they fled. It was a disgrace to be caught. I recall being awakened at two or three in the morning by the firing of shots.

New Year's Eve was also a time for pranks. There was usually no destruction of property. We had visited the J. C. Jensen family and when we came home about midnight the hayrack was standing in front of the house. It was not easy to get into the house. The fellows had entered the house and had put some gunpowder into father's tobacco, and had removed some slats from some of the beds. Next morning we discovered that the wheels from a farm wagon were missing. Later we found a wheel at each of the four corners of our home farm. Father did not exactly appreciate their sense of humor.

This Jensen family meant most to us in my childhood. Mary Jensen and mother were very close friends. Having much in common, they shared both joys and sorrows. How often I was sent over there to borrow some baking powder or a dry yeast cake. That dear woman always gave me a cookie or something when I came.

Father and J. C. were also good friends. They helped each other in haying, harvest, and with many other jobs.

In those days we did not do any shock threshing. We always stacked our grain. We children all pitched in and helped where we could. Father and J. C. carried on a constant barrage of kidding and joking. I never saw two men have so much fun together, and we children enjoyed it all. I might add that this mutual aid was in part social. These pioneers helped each other with so many things that we American-born later thought of it as being a bit silly.

We children also helped each other. When the grass was short in the pastures, and that was often true in summer, we herded our cattle together on the roads. We walked together to school and played after school.

We two families visited each other at least once a week. There was no telephone, so on an evening the one family simply went to vist the other. Our parents were soon playing cards and they had a good time doing that. I might add that there was considerable card playing in our neighborhood, but I never saw anybody do any gambling.

We children were sent to another room in the house. We, too, played simple card games. In our games there was a constant uproar. To be heard one had to shout at the top of his voice. Soon everybody was shouting. From time to time one of the women came to restore order. It was successful for a while. Little by little sleep put its demands upon us, and one after the other would go off by himself and find a suitable place and fall asleep. By the time our parents were ready to go home, we, many children, were scattered all over the place. In our family there were eight children and the Jensens had at least ten, so to find them all was not so easy, and to wake them up was a job. J. C. used to say about me that I was the only person he had ever seen who could stand up and be fast asleep.

Edward and I did our best to make a kite that would fly. We must have made them by the scores, but they refused to get very far off the earth. If one of them did rise to a hundred feet or more, it usually came down with a crash and was no more.

One day father brought me a kite from town. It was

a marvelous creation. I am sure that I was the proudest and the happiest boy in our neighborhood. That thing could go up so high that I could hardly see it. As soon as I had really learned to fly it, I was going over to the Jensens to exhibit it. Mother called for supper, but I told her that I was too busy to eat. She insisted. I laid the kite on a box outside the house and put a small weight on it. While I was eating, a gust of wind blew my divine kite into the pig yard and they devoured it. What this meant to a ten-year-old boy cannot be told. I never did get another kite that would fly, and after that I never liked pigs.

VII

SOME COMMUNITY ACTIVITIES

I am a tiller of the soil,*
A farmer frank and plain;
I love my home, its life and toil,
Its fields and wooded lane,
There countless flowers are growing
In beauty rich and rare;
Mine is the brooklet flowing,
And mine the fragrant air.

This poem was written by the Danish farmer, Mads Hansen, about a century ago, and translated by the Rev. J. C. Aaberg. Here is expressed the farmer's love of his home and his work. Most of the farmers of our community knew this song, and I am sure, agreed with its sentiment.

The farmers in our community were in appearance rugged individualists. The men who ran things were in the prime of life. When the farmers came together for their

* See WORLD OF SONG, Grand View College, Des Moines, Iowa.

meetings they were certainly an odd looking group. They were nearly all dressed in brown or blue jeans. Since safety razors were still unknown and shaving an ordeal, most of the men wore beards. There were long beards and short beards, clean beards and dirty beards, forked beards and fan-shaped beards. Then there was an array of mustaches that would have gladdened the heart of a Grant Wood. There were those of a Kaiser William II or of a Louis Napoleon III. There was the walrus kind and those that grew completely wild.

Most of these men had bought their land at a low price, and prudent and thrifty Danes made it a point to pay debts when crops and prices were good. This made them financially independent. Such farmers could look a money lender straight in the face and tell him that they were going to vote the Populist ticket in the next election. There were a few Civil War veterans who found it expedient to become Republicans. It helped them to get soldiers' pension, so the story went. These farmers paraded in the Alliance movement and voted for Bryan and his Sixteen to One. They hated the railroads and felt that they were being robbed by bankers, middlemen and corporations. One of our neighbors was so violently partisan that he openly rejoiced when President William McKinley was assassinated in 1901. However, this attitude shocked many people.

On a whole, I would say that these immigrant farmers were fully as well posted and more intellectually alert than most farmers of our day. They turned out in large numbers to hear political speakers. Father, mother and many others drove the long way to Grand Island to hear William Jennings Bryan in 1896. They came home with greater enthusiasm than ever for the Great Commoner. One of our neighbors was so interested in books that he would tie his team to a fence post and go home and read the great Soren Kirkegaard. In the meantime corn and weeds were left to fight it out. Too often the weeds won the day. He maintained that mental weeds were the more dangerous and should have first attention.

The political campaign of 1896 was one of the liveliest and the hottest I can remember. Father and most of our neighbors were Populists or Bryan Democrats. There were many well-attended meetings. It seems that the Democrats had the enthusiasm and the Republicans the propaganda. Our county was flooded with cartoons and leaflets. Since there were not many Republicans in our school district, any child who was not enthusiastic for Bryan was suspected of being a Gold Republican, and was brain-washed. I do not recall anything about election day, but on the following day we school children, on the way home from school, met a man on a load of hay. We cried to him, "Hurrah for Bryan!"

He replied, "Hurrah for Bryan! McKinley is elected!" We continued our way home with heavy hearts and told our parents the sad news. It was also their first election returns.

In connection with politics it should be mentioned that there was one political office in the county which was filled by a Dane as far back as I can remember, and that was the office of county treasurer. The Danes did not think they had much use for a county judge or a county attorney, but they had to do business with the treasurer. Taxes were always with them. In this office they wanted a man whom they knew and could trust. Furthermore, they wanted a man with whom they could speak their mother tongue. Peter Ebbesen was such a man and was the county treasurer for many years.

These farmers came from a country where the co-operatives were already strong when they left. It was natural for them to carry the movement to this country. They organized co-operative elevators, lumber yards, shipping associations, creameries and credit associations. During the early years they co-operated very well, but as time went on that spirit weakened. A good co-op man is a man with foresight. The man who lacks that will save a dime today and lose many dollars in years to come.

The pioneers in our community were cultural individualists and economic collectivists. They knew that they stood and fell together. As time went on, these farmers tended to become cultural collectivists and economic individualists. The result was that in place of supporting their own projects loyally, they went and bought their goods where they could get them a trifle cheaper and thereby ruined their own associations. Their enemies won the day by applying the ancient practice of Divide and Rule.

Some farmers had organized a savings bank at Nysted. Men who had a little money to spare would put it there, and trusted men who needed short-term loans could borrow much more cheaply than at a regular bank.

One year a rumor was circulating that this savings bank was going to be robbed. Word came to father about this and he was asked to come to the village that night to protect the community financial institution. After supper father took his shotgun and got ready to go. I asked him if I might go with him, and strangely enough he gave his consent.

The manager of this little bank was Kristian Jensen. He and his faithful little wife had retired from farm life very early. I suspect one reason was that he disliked physical labor. He was an interesting man with an inquiring mind. His hobby was reading and he was the local authority on the French Revolution. My oldest sister, Anna, married their son, Julius.

When father and I arrived at the home of Kristian Jensen, it seemed to me that I could see that he was agitated. A bold bank robbery was not a trifling matter. There were a half dozen farmers present, each with his shotgun or rifle. They arranged themselves into shifts to keep an eye on suspicious looking visitors. At every strange sound, the guard would give a start. This was really exciting. I was hoping for some action like the great battles of Lexington and Concord where the embattled farmers won immortality. But the night grew more and more quiet and I more and more sleepy. When father awakened me it was after midnight and we set out on foot for home. On the way home, I asked father, "Was your gun really loaded?" He did not say much in reply. I doubt that it was.

The farmers were also rough and ready when it came to taking action. One year a gang of horse riders from a distance tried to terrorize the neighborhood. They rode up and down the roads and into the towns at full speed firing revolvers into the air. Frank and Jesse James were their idols. One day my brother, Chris, and I were walking through a hay field, when three of these riders came along the road at full speed. We crouched low in the tall prairie grass, and after firing a few shots, the men on their horses disappeared in a cloud of dust.

These fellows took a special delight in breaking up country dances. They would make their appearance when a dance was well started and walk into the hall in full regalia, including revolvers, boots, spurs, and cowboy hats. But they carried this a bit too far.

A few of the more husky farmers decided that this was enough. One evening when there was a dance at Nysted they decided to do something. They were there waiting for the bullies. At about ten o'clock the horsemen came down the road at full speed, shooting and shouting. They tied up their horses to the hitching posts and came swaggering into the hall. They had consumed just enough liquor to make themselves brave. They began to take charge of things. Just then a half-dozen horny-fisted farmers stepped into the building, rope in hand, caught the three budding Al Capones, hog-tied them and threw them into a hog wagon. One of the bullies cried for mercy, but resolutely the farmers hauled them to the county seat where they were thrown into jail. That was the last of the night riders.

But there were also trolls and evil spirits among the Danes. A mile to the south of my home lived a childless couple, Mr. and Mrs. Charley Sorensen. He was a kindly man. He had had the misfortune to lose a hand in a corn shredder. In place of this, he wore a steel hook which to me looked cold and cruel. His wife was not Danish and that was a handicap in the community. She seemed sullen and ugly of mind and soul. She was surely a kleptomaniac and perhaps a pyromaniac. They did not quite belong in the community.

Having much work to do and no children to help them, they adopted a little boy, whose name was Fred. The poor fellow was about six when he entered that gloomy home. People felt sorry for the boy and soon stories were being told of how cruelly he was treated. He frequently had severe scalp wounds, and it was generally believed that these were caused by the beatings of this wicked woman.

Fred must have been treated harshly for it was discovered that he preferred sleeping in an abandoned barn to going home to his foster parents. He came to school without food and the other children shared their lunches with him. This condition could not go on indefinitely. One evening after school, the J. C. Jensen family asked Fred to come to their home for supper. They had not asked the permission of the unhappy boy's parents. He was so happy that they decided to keep him overnight. He went with their children to school the next day, and with them home again in the evening. That the Jensens had taken Fred into their home, was the talk of the school and the community. Charley Sorensens had also learned where their boy was staying.

That evening there happened to be a birthday party at the Niels Hermansen home. J. C. Jensens went to the party and took Fred with them. In the meantime, Charley Sorensens had learned that Fred was at the Hermansen party. Mr. Sorensen and his husky hired man went there. First they went to the kitchen door and knocked. Mrs. Hermansen opened the door. When she saw who was at the door, she became excited and slapped Mr. Sorensen in the face with a dish towel, which she happened to have in her hand. The two men retreated before this display of feminine wrath and went to the front door and knocked. By this time all knew who was there. Mr. Hermansen and Louis Sorensen, the brother of Charley Sorensen, both went to the door. When Charley saw his brother, he winced, turned pale, and asked him if he too was against him. Whereupon Louis replied that he was against the boy being abused. After this uncomfortable little incident, Charley Sorensen asked Mr. Hermansen if his boy was in the house. He told him that he was. Mr. Sorensen then said, "If you don't give up my boy peacefully, there will be trouble." After a short conference, while the two men were still on the porch, it was decided that Fred would have to go with them. When the boy heard this, he screamed loudly, and pleaded with the Jensens to rescue him. By force the boy was turned over to Charley Sorensen, and Louis Sorensen told his brother to be good to the boy. As the sobbing boy was being carried away, there was a stunned silence in the house, and all went to their homes.

Later court proceedings were started and Mr. and Mrs. Charley Sorensen were compelled to give up Fred. He was adopted by another couple and became a good Dane.

Mrs. Charley Sorensen seemed to have the idea that her brother-in-law, Louis Sorensen, was back of the movement to take their boy away from them. There may also have been an element of jealousy. The Louis Sorensens were respected and the Charley Sorensens were not.

Some time later Mr. and Mrs. Louis Sorensen began to receive anonymous letters. They contained the most dire threats and were vile and venomous beyond description. These good people were most unhappy, and it was the common opinion among the neighbors that Mrs. Charley Sorensen had written and sent them.

One Sunday there was a church meeting at Nysted and Louis Sorensens were there. During a recess in the afternoon, smoke was seen rising to the skies toward the southeast. As if fearing something, Louis Sorensen immediately climbed a windmill tower and shouted, "Friends, my house is burning." To the church barns rushed scores of men and soon riders and drivers were hurrying down the road. Some of the boys ran across the fields. It was too late. The house with most of its contents burned to the ground. There was no rural fire department.

Since the Sorensens had left home before ten in the morning, and this was at least five hours later, it was generally believed that the fire had been set by an enemy of the family. All knew who that was.

One late summer evening, Chris and I set out from Dannebrog. We had attended a tent show in the village square. Other young people from our community were there too. As I recall it, we had seen **Ten Nights in a Bar Room** and had been properly impressed.

As we drove over the hills west of town toward home, we noticed some reflections of fire in the western skies. In the beginning we paid little attention to them, but as the skies became brighter, we drove faster. When we reached the last hill before entering the Oak Creek valley of the Nysted community, we saw that it was Louis Sorensen's grain stacks that were burning. There were two fires as there were two settings of stacks. When we arrived, there were many people present, and they were busy carrying grain bundles away from the fire. The whole Louis Sorensen family was there, and naturally depressed. Their grain harvest was nearly a total loss, and then there was the haunting fear of the unseen enemy.

Since there had been no lightning, and nobody had been working near the grain stacks, it was obvious that the fire was the work of an arsonist.

I noticed that most of the farmers had a conference when the fires were low. Father did not tell us what it was about.

Next day a delegation from the neighborhood set out for St. Paul to see the county attorney. While they had no direct evidence, they did tell the attorney that they knew who had done the foul deeds. After a long conference, the attorney told them that it was not possible to prosecute a person on such evidence.

There was much talk of bloodhounds, but nothing came of that. However, not many days later, men on foot, on horseback and in buggies began to gather at the Charley Sorensen home. It was a community mass demonstration. As the crowd approached the house, they saw that the evil woman was sitting on the front porch. She had undoubtedly seen the crowd and went out to meet them, rather than have them come into the house. The people moved up to the porch. I was with father and kept close to him. I was afraid. I had heard so many stories about this witch, and I was convinced that half was not known about her evil deeds. There she sat brazenly peeling potatoes, and the way she brandished that butcher knife was enough to make a boy snuggle up to his dad for protection.

As the crowd gathered about the porch, she did not look up, but worked with a frenzied determination. The spokesman, an attorney, now stepped up toward her and said something like this, "We have come to let you know that you are not wanted in this community. That is why we are here. We want you to get out and stay out. This is the sentiment of all your neighbors. The sooner you people leave, the happier we will be."

She retorted with some sharp words after which the leader told her that they had been sufficiently warned.

Her husband had not been at home during this demonstration. It must have been an ordeal for her. However, something must have been accomplished. There were no more threatening letters and no more mysterious fires. About a year later, the unpopular couple left for the west, never to return.

One summer was very wet and the rains continued into the late fall. We had not been able to get our grain threshed and father and several neighbors became very impatient. They finally became so tired of waiting that they decided to buy their own threshing machine. This machine was horsepower driven. When the machine was bought, I was too young to go threshing. There were perhaps about a dozen farmers in this threshing ring.

The threshing machine was moved from place to place by horses. It took a good team to pull the machine through a soft stubble field. Some times it was necessary to have four horses hitched to it. It took some skill to set a threshing machine. It was pulled between the stacks. There were usually four stacks in a setting. The machine had to be set quite level. There was trouble if it was not. There must not be too much vibration so each of the four wheels was lowered into a small hole. Our machine did not have a blower to get rid of the straw. It had a straw carrier. This thing had revolving slats that carried the straw away from the machine and into the stack.

It also took skill to set the horsepower correctly. It had to be lined up with the thresher and just the right distance from it. Then the horsepower was anchored so that it would not move when the horses went round and round. Anchoring the machine was not easy. Rods were hooked to the horsepower and fastened to the ground by means of stakes. It took skill to drive these stakes into the ground just right. Usually these stakes were made of a tough wood. Two or three men would get on a stake with a sledge hammer and what pride the farm boys took in their ability to use a sledge hammer. When the horsepower was set securely, the tumbling rods were put in place. These were shafts with joints that extended from the horsepower to the threshing machine and through these rods came the power that turned the thresher. When the rods were in place, the five teams were hitched on to the sweeps which were heavy timbers that extended out from the power. When the man who tended the threshing machine gave the signal, a man climbed onto the horsepower, two men went to the top of two grain stacks, a wagon was backed up to the grain spout and two men got ready to take care of the straw stack. Another signal was given and the man on the horsepower told the horses to "Get Up." He had a long whip and if necessary let the lazy among the horses have it. The machine started slowly and it took some time to get up full speed. When it had that speed, the boss gave the men in the grain stacks the signal and they began to pitch bundles into the machine. This, too, required some care. They were to be thrown in head first, and not too fast and not too slowly. Good stack pitchers were important if a good threshing job was to be done.

The men who took care of setting the straw had a

dirty job. It was often very dusty and it was hard work. One man threw the straw back from the carrier and the other took care of the size and shape of the straw stack. There were usually two men who hauled the threshed grain to the storage bin. There were no elevators then and the men threw the grain into the bin with grain shovels.

Threshing was an important activity on our farm. Everybody was busy. Mother and the girls prepared three meals a day for all these men and they were hearty eaters. The activity began before daybreak and lasted till it was dark in the evening. It could also be a happy time. How thankful my parents were when we got a good harvest! It often took a couple of days to finish threshing our grain. We were glad when the threshers came and glad when they left. It was hard for me to go to school when we threshed. I was happy when my parents would let me stay home those days.

While it was hard work to make the rounds with the threshing machine, the young fellows liked it. There was good food and lots of it. Furthermore the fellows had a lot of fun together.

The first steam driven thresher I recall was one owned by Herman Hermansen. He was a brother of Niels and Martin Hermansen.

All of these Hermansens were, of course, born in Denmark. One by one the boys left for America. Herman being the oldest of the children had inherited the family farm. He was well educated. He had attended both folk schools and agricultural schools in Denmark. He married the daughter of a wealthy farmer.

Now that all his brothers were in the New World, he must have received letters telling about the wonders of the New World. He, too, decided to emigrate and came to the Nysted community with his family and his money in 1881.

He bought a big farm. He built excellent buildings and had beauty about the place. He and his wife entertained royally. Their home was a social center. He was active in community affairs. He had money and that always attracts fine friends. He had many of them. These fine friends surely flattered him for it is said that when he had imbibed too much, he did not recognize his more common neighbors.

He built a creamery and in it had the latest and best machinery. He had many milk and cream routes. Things were done in a big way, perhaps too big for efficiency. It is said that Hermansen was away from home too much; and in human affairs, too, when the cats are away the mice play. One dark night the creamery burned.

It was a community sensation when he bought a steam engine and a threshing machine. This was really big. But a steam engine can be as balky as a mule. Nobody knew how to run the thing. There was the simple problem of keeping up steam and that proved to be not so simple. Hermansen became desperate and drove to St. Paul to find an engineer. He found a man by the name of Mr. Bebe. He had run a stationery engine successfully. He should be able to run an engine on wheels. He was brought out to Nysted and the little people must have been impressed with this expert. But his reputation must have been greater than his skill. He, too, could not keep up steam. Steam is power and you can't thresh without power. They had to stop quite often while Bebe got up steam again.

Much money had been invested in this outfit and something had to be done. Finally Hermansen decided to send his son, Peter, to an engineering school. He later came back with knowledge and skill. He took over the job as engineer of the balky engine and Peter could keep up steam. Now for a good threshing run!

However, man is born to trouble as the sparks fly upward, says the Good Book, and the sparks flew upward from Hermansen's engine too. A steam engine is heavy and there were many bridges over the numerous creeks in Howard County. Bridges in those days were not built by graduates of engineering colleges. Just about anybody could build a bridge across Oak Creek and anybody did.

71

One day Peter Hermansen and his helper came to the Melsen bridge near Dannebrog. That bridge did not look very strong. To play safe, they hauled the threshing machine across with a team of horses and the driver warned them that the bridge was weak. They started the engine across and the bridge gave way with a horrible crash. Peter jumped for his life and made it. The other man at the steering wheel went down with engine and bridge. The water was deep, but he managed to keep his mouth above it till he was freed.

The engine was later removed from the murky waters, but at that it was a heavy loss for Mr. Hermansen. However, that was not all. The country was sinking into a depression; the serious one of the nineties. Hermansen sank deeper and deeper into financial troubles. He had a big sale and left for a new Danish settlement in Texas called Dannevang.... Sic transit gloria mundi.

It is not easy for a person who has not lived on a farm to conceive what a misfortune it is to lose a harvest. Looking in vain for rain was a large part of life in Howard County. That unpleasant experience marked a person for life. In the roughly forty-five years that father was a farmer it is doubtful that he got a corn crop every other year.

For years, when there was a drouth, we cut the dry corn stalks by hand and put them into shocks. But as a feed for cattle this was not very satisfactory.

Some time early in this century father read in **Wallaces Farmer** about silos and how farmers cut corn stalks into silage and stored this green fodder in huge bins called silos. But silos were very expensive. Some years later he read about pit silos. It seemed that if there was a good clay soil a hole could be dug in the ground and the corn silage stored there.

One summer there was promise of a good corn crop, but then early in August hot winds blew across the plains from the southwest. Father could see that the corn would not last long in that extreme heat. Louis Sorensen, our neighbor, was a handy man, who could make most anything. He and father talked about digging a pit silo. Louis invented the necessary apparatus and all went to work.

A cable was suspended above the place where the pit silo would be dug. A box was lowered into the hole, where two or three workers filled it with dirt and a horse pulled the loaded box out of the hole. Louis Sorensen had supervision of all the machinery and the work. Holger and Ferdinand Sorensen drove the horse and three of us did the digging. While it was hard work, it was not long till we had a pit silo on the Louis Sorensen farm and one on our farm. It was, of course, dangerous for the diggers to stand in that deep hole as the big box loaded with heavy dirt was hoisted out. However, we had no accidents and it was fun working with other fellows. Our silo was twenty feet deep and ten feet in diameter. When the hole was finished, the walls of the silo were plastered with cement. About three feet at the top were bricked up. Louis Sorensen did that work.

As soon as the silos were completed, we began to fill them. We used a corn binder to cut the stalks and at the silo we had a small silage cutter pulled by a gasoline engine. As the silage scattered all about the place, Louis Sorensen made a tube of gunny sacks so the flow of the silage could be controlled. Since the corn stalks were too dry, we added some water to the silage.

This feed was much better than the dry corn stalks and in a few years there were many pit silos in the community.

VIII

SCHOOL DAYS

The Nysted church maintained what was called a vacation school for us children. The children attended the school until they began to receive instruction for confirmation. It was held during the months of May and June. Our parents took us out of the common school during May. However, all the children of the common school did not attend the vacation school.

The aim of this school was not only religious instruction, but also to teach the cultural heritage of Denmark. It was a wise thing as it helped to bring children and parents closer together. While we children were not very conscious of the fact that our parents were foreigners, the vacation school did help us to appreciate the things our parents held dear.

Usually the teachers in the vacation school were better educated than the teachers in the public schools. Most of them had received their education in Denmark and had been influenced by the folk school ideas. The language used for instruction was, of course, Danish. Furthermore, the teachers asked us to use that language on the playground. But here the high cultural individualism of the Danes becames evident. The children insisted on their constitutional right to speak the American language while at play.

When we began school all of us could speak the Danish language. It was not long till we could read Danish stories. We read them eagerly. They seemed more interesting than most of the stories in our American text books.

For me this vacation school was a rich experience. We children loved to sing the beautiful Danish songs. There were scores of them, songs for all occasions, and we sang them with delight.

The best thing about this school was the story hour. The teachers did not read the stories. He or she knew that a story is more effective if it is well told. There were Bible stories and stories of Danish heroes from history. There were stories of the old Norse gods and we had Thor and Odin pictured so vividly to us that we could see Thor throw his hammer and hear him dashing across the skies, causing the roll of thunder.

When I think of the vacation school, one teacher always comes to my mind. His name was R. J. Martensen. He was an excellent story teller. While any story he told was certain to be good, he did excel in telling the fairy tales of Hans Christian Andersen. How we laughed when he told the story of Big Claus and Little Claus. On the other hand, it was difficult to keep back the tears when he told the story of the mother whose only child was taken by the Grim Reaper, and how she was willing to give all to get it back, and even to go to the end of the world. Then there was the sad, sad story of the little match girl. I can see the teacher as he stood almost transfigured by the joy of telling a story to eager listeners. This was vitalized education.

But if the teacher were not a good story teller, there could be trouble. One such teacher was a cripple and was a good deal of a bore. One day he was telling a dull story and I was paying no attention. I was in the land of dreams where I loved to be. Suddenly Victor Hermansen began reaching into the air as if he were grabbing something. The teacher stopped and said, "Victor, what are you doing?"

Victor replied without a smile, "Sir, I am catching your words." The story hour ended in an uproar.

Our public school was a two-room brick building situated a half mile east of Nysted. The whole place was ill-kept. In dry weather the dust flew in clouds. In rainy weather the yard was a sea of mud. The interior of the building had nothing to inspire awe or respect. The only picture was a faded print of the Statue of Liberty. Tattered maps hung on the grimy walls. The floor was worn white and rough. The double desks were filled with ancient carvings that would have gladdened the heart of an archeologist. The old heating stove was red with rust and the glow of by-gone fires. There was no library. The books available for the pupils were old, uninteresting texts. There was, however, a large dictionary, the most interesting book there.

The other buildings on the grounds consisted of two privies and a coal shed. All cried to high heaven for paint, but most of the time their prayers went unheeded. The privies were the object of violence at least once a year. When New Year's Eve came along, they were sure to be tipped over and lay there till the local school board restored them to their proper position.

If there was poverty in the way of equipment and appearance, there was no want in the number of children. At times ninety children were enrolled. They all walked to school. None was mad enough to suggest that children should be spoiled by hauling them to school in wagons, and enclosed buses were unknown. Some of the pupils walked nearly three miles. In zero weather this could be trying. In those days, children started school at six or seven. During the winter months, when farm work was slack, it was not unusual to see boys and girls in school who were sixteen and seventeen years of age and often taller than the teacher. There was no graduation from the eighth grade. In fact no pupil was quite sure which grade he was in. He just went to school.

Practically all the children in school were of Danish parentage. During recess the children spoke Danish and no teacher possessed enough authority to stop it. It was the language of the homes, and most of the children could speak nothing but that when they started school. However, the teachers were patient about the language question. They earned their meager salaries in a Danish community and prudence dictated that they treat their employers with respect.

The teachers were for the most part sincere even if poorly prepared. Most of them belonged to the type Professor Hugo Munsterberg spoke of as being "A mob of mobile maidens meditating matrimony." When the maidens had too much trouble maintaining order, a man would be hired who wielded the rod with expert efficiency.

Some used the most ingenious devices to instill fear into the hearts of their unwilling pupils. One, a large man, had the habit of keeping a supply of erasers conveniently at hand and hurling them at offenders. He could hurl a missile with the accuracy of a William Tell, and many a boy had a bump on his cranium as proof. If a wood-back eraser failed to restore order, he had a strong stick on his desk which he used freely and effectively.

One year the children in the upper room became so unruly that things were on the verge of chaos, and at times completely so. To this day, I am not able to explain the causes. The teacher that unhappy year was Mr. J. Fredriksen.* He had taught successfully in both folk school and the vacation school. He had not taught in a public school before. He was a kind man and much better educated than most of our teachers, but we were not interested or impressed by his superior fund of knowledge. He was guilty of several innovations which we did not like; among them was his habit of starting the school day with a long period of devotions. We had no abstract theories as to the necessity of keeping church and school in full and complete separation, but other teachers had not prayed for the eternal salvation of our souls and that was enough. One morning the opposition was thoroughly organized. Every pupil had been instructed, and anyone refusing to co-operate was threatened with dire and terrible consequences. When Mr. Fredriksen came to the end of his long prayer, the whole class joined him in a loud "Amen". Following this demonstration, he announced sternly that we would all join in singing, "While the Morning

* Fictitious name.

Bells are Ringing." He began and not a voice joined him. Painfully, he sang the first stanza, while the whole class listened, the more timid girls with fear and the braver boys with triumph. He stopped and demanded that we all take part. With some nervousness, he started the second stanza. The non-co-operation plan worked perfectly. Gandhi never had better success. When he had finished the second stanza, he announced that we would take up our studies.

The studies were taken up and with great reluctance. Mischief was in the air. Boys brought ripe hackberries to school and scattered them on the floor, and when one was stepped on it gave a loud crack. When a class was asked to come forward to the long recitation seat, every one of the boys would have several of the berries under his shoes and there was a crack, crack. Boys brought cartridges to school, rolled them in paper and dropped them in paper baskets or the coal bucket. When these were emptied into the stove, there was enough noise to make it sound like modern bombing. When mud was carried into the schoolroom on our shoes, mud balls flew thick and fast. When mud was not in season, paper balls were used.

Trouble dogged the poor man's life. Could he have been free of it during recess, it might not have been so bad, but he was not spared. He was continually fighting organized rebellion. One day a wet snow fell. It was perfect for snowballs. The boys went out into the road and piled up the ammunition. When there was an adequate supply, snowballs began to fly against the schoolhouse and in the open door. The teacher appeared in the door and demanded that this be stopped at once. It was not. He walked over toward the rebels, and one of the leaders said to the other boys crouched low behind the fence, "Hold your fire until you can see the white of his eyes and then let him have it." This was a second Bunker Hill, only this time the rebels did not run out of ammunition. They waited and on the signal, the air was thick with rockets, missiles and snowballs. The unhappy man made a quick about face and beat a hasty retreat. One missile hit his cap and tilted it at a silly angle, but there was no time to maintain dignity or to think about appearances. Without another word, he retired behind the doors of his house of sorrows. He had both mental and physical wounds.

About a half mile from the school, was a small pond. When the ice was good, the children went there during the noon hour. No one had a watch and none cared if the time went past the time for classes. The schoolmaster would appear on the hill and wave his arms wildly and ring the hand bell frantically. It took time for his mentally reluctant pupils to reach the school again.

On certain days, conditions approached anarchy. The poor man would then resort to physical punishment, mostly in the form of a violent slap on the side of the face. When one of the boys received a much deserved and resounding whack, the other boys would laugh raucously.

One afternoon Mr. Fredriksen's patience had reached exhaustion and he dismissed the school, but asked two of us to remain in our seats. I was badly frightened and was certain that I would receive the whipping I knew I deserved. However, I was spared the ordeal, but Tom Hermansen got a haymaker on the side of his face. The other boys, instead of going home as they had been told to do, gathered at the windows outside the building to cheer us on in our hour of trial. He tried to chase the boys away, but with no success. When he failed, he dismissed us. As Tom walked out of the door, he turned and said to his teacher, "Mr. Fredriksen, you may go to grass."

He complained to our parents. I overheard my father tell him that it was his job to teach the school and to keep order, and if his boys did not behave themselves, he should give them the punishment they needed. The school board intervened and pleaded with the boys, but the whole situation was out of control and it was not cured till the teacher quit.

In many ways the pioneer farmers were generous, and at times, perhaps generous to a fault. One of our neighbors, Mr. and Mrs. Chris Christensen, had a daughter who had a horrible lung disease. I suspect it was tuberculosis. This poor girl went to school with us when she was well enough to do so. She breathed the same foul air and drank from the same water dipper. She had a most terrible cough, and when she had coughed for some time, she would have to rush outside to vomit. Very often she could not hold back the vomit and it spilled on the floor. Then there was an almost unbearable stench in the room. Outside the school door there was a green mound of her vomit. During the spring and fall, this was covered with hundreds of flies. We made life hard for this pathetic child. In her presence, we held our noses and told her that she was a stinker. We did not want to sit next to her, and during recess none would play with her. She cried and her mother often rebuked some of us. Maybe we children were acting in self-defense. We complained to our parents that the stench about her was too much. Their reply was that we must be kind to the child. She continued in our school till her parents moved away.

There is an old adage that tells us that forbidden fruit is sweet. One thing that was forbidden children was the use of matches. The danger of fire on the usually dry prairies was very great. One evening the teacher asked Edward and me to sweep out the school for her after dismissal time. We consented. When all the children had left and we had swept out the school, we found the key for her desk and ransacked it. In it was a box of matches and we took some. We locked the desk carefully and put the key back into its very secret place, locked the school door and set out for home. The matches in our pockets bothered us. They seemed hot and we wanted to use them. As we walked down the hill toward the Larsen bridge, we met a lady driving in a top buggy. I recognized her, but I felt sure that she did not know me. I noticed that she had some dry hay tucked in behind the seat of her buggy. The top was up, and I was sure she could not see me, so I ran up from behind and pulled out the hay. She stopped short and cried in a shrill voice, "I know you. You are one of Rasmus

Nielsen's bad boys. I will tell your father on you." Then she drove on. What a burden it was that mischievous boys were known throughout the community.

Edward and I now had a conference. We had an armful of dry hay and plenty of matches. But it was a dry, windy spring day and we would have to be careful that the fire did not get away from us. We decided that the safest place to have a little bonfire was under the wooden bridge. We put the stolen hay there and then gathered some dry weeds till we had quite a pile. We then set fire to it. The fire took hold and what a smoke there was! We had not considered that. It came out from under the bridge in huge, black billows. We tried to stamp it out. It was too strong. I was terrified. The wooden bridge might catch fire. To add to my dismay, I saw that a man came running toward us from the Larsen home. There was no escape. Lars Larsen recognized both of us and shouted, "What are you boys doing on a day like this?" We pleaded guilty. He managed to put out the fire and no damage was done. He gave us a lecture. We stood in his presence, meek and lowly. He told us to go home. We were glad to get away. On the way there we got rid of the matches. We did not dare to use them. It seems that we drowned them in a small puddle of water.

Very meekly, I came home. I wondered if anyone had seen the fire or the smoke. Thank goodness no one said anything. I was safe. But the bottom went out of my self-confidence when mother told me to hurry up with the chores, that we were all going up to Larsens for a birthday party after supper. Had she observed me carefully she would surely have seen that her son was in despair!

Ordinarily I liked to go to Larsens. It was the only home in our community which had a piano, and I liked music.

When we entered the Larsen home, there stood Lars, with what I thought was a gloating grin. I shook hands with him. He must have seen my great distress. He never said any more about it.

As mentioned earlier, the language on the school grounds was generally Danish. We children could be as cruel as children often are. A Polish family moved into our district. They had many children and these were well behaved and were better dressed than most of us. But they were not Danish and that was enough. We were against them. For at least a year, we boys did not permit the Polish boys to play with us. They could get their fun and exercise watching us. We were their superiors and we wanted them to know it.

But we did not confine our persecution to non-Danes. Anybody was welcome to our sadism. One fall a boy enrolled in our school. He had a Danish name, but we did not think he quite looked like one. His head was big, and the one eye was larger than the other, and the small one was not quite in focus. He was not clever and he was alone.

We were sure he needed our attention and he got it. We tormented him with words. He was slow on the trigger. One boy would push another boy against him. He did not say anything to our tormenting and bullying.

One evening after school, he caught me alone. My bravery vanished. I had no audience. I was much smaller than he, and words were no weapons against his superior strength. He threw me hard to the ground several times. He boxed my ears. In my anguish, I cried for help. Sofie Jensen heard my cries and came. She ruined a perfectly good lunch pail on his rear end. He left me whimpering on the ground. Other children came and saw a fallen hero. I cried all the way home from school. Mother's only remark was, "You probably got just what you deserved."

When I was about ten years old, two families moved into our district whose children could not speak Danish. These families came to us with some prestige and the language of our playground gradually changed. Our first language became the American, and this meant that we learned to speak the language of the land without an accent.

This was not true of the older children of our community.

One cause for the discipline problem in our school was the fact that there was not enough work for us. There were no or few interesting books. As mentioned above, we did have a large dictionary, and I literally spent hours looking at the pictures and illustrations in it. Many of us children were mentally hungry, but there was not enough material to satisfy us.

However, each year was not a wasteland. The fact that education was poorly organized from above gave good teachers a chance to teach the things in which they excelled and which they loved. There were no eighth grade examinations for which to drill. When I look back at this school with its spelling-down contests, etc., I am inclined to believe that we learned the fundamentals about as well as children do now.

Then, too, there are some advantages in having several grades in the same room. We who sat in our seats learned something from hearing class after class read great and good stories. We even learned some arithmetic by seeing advanced problems done on the blackboard.

We had one teacher whose soul was full of poetry. She read poetry so beautifully that I shall not forget it. She read good books to us by the hour. There were also teachers who loved good music. They taught us songs that are still with us.

However, the best work done by the Little Red Schoolhouse all over the land was not in reading and writing and arithmetic, important as that was. The most important work done was **E Pluribus Unum**. It was done with little or no fanfare. There was no oath taking and no ceremonial flag raising. It was done quietly and effectively in thousands of schools and the people hardly knew that the process was going on.

For a thousand years my people had lived among the lakes and hills of Jutland, Denmark. Some of the well-meaning, if misguided, teachers of the vacation school had told us that we owed our first allegiance to Denmark.

We did not argue with them. We hardly gave the statement any thought. But lo, something was happening in the deep recesses of our minds. When we children played war on the playgrounds, we were not divided between Danes and Germans. Most of these children had ancestors who had fought the Germans. No! We fought the battles of Lexington, Bunker Hill, Gettysburg and San Juan Hill over again. In most of our war games we were divided between the Patriots and the Redcoats, and God loved the Patriots under the leadership of George Washington and they won the day.

Children of Polish, Swedish, German, Norwegian, Irish, Italian and Finnish parents all over the land in public schools were going through the same experience. They were becoming Americans. These many nations of the world were becoming one nation: American, and there were no cheers. That work had to be done and the Little Red Schoolhouse did it so well that the American people today are among the most loyal in the world.

In Europe they have tried to force assimilation and loyalty and they have failed. Germany tried hard, but could not make patriotic Germans out of Poles, Frenchmen and Danes; and Russia failed miserably in her attempt to assimilate the Poles. In America we used the voluntary method and we succeeded beyond all expectations. This should be a capital lesson for all those who are willing to learn.

IX
IN THE SHADOW OF THE CHURCH

Through the years the Nysted church and the folk school continued to do their work. My sister, Anna, attended the school while Pastor Strandskov was the headmaster. She was very enthusiastic about her experience there. But as mentioned earlier times were hard in the nineties, and it was difficult to get enough students to keep the school going.

I played with the Strandskov children. Uffe had a tricycle and I was sure that he was the happiest boy in the land. The Strandskov children had a most impressive swing. Two rope swings were tied to a wooden frame and on these two swings was placed a wooden plank. Several children could swing at once. What a luxury this was. Most of us were fortunate if we had a simple swing from the branch of a tree.

The Strandskovs left Nysted in 1898. Why they left, I do not know, but I can imagine that the cares of church and school were too much for them. The Nysted people were sorry to see them leave. Pastor Strandskov accepted a call from a larger congregation near Marquette, Nebraska.

The next man to become the pastor of the Nysted church and headmaster of the folk school was Rev. Thorvald Knudsen. He was a handsome man with grey eyes and a finely built face. His complexion was most fair. He was medium in height, with natural dignity. His personality was one of the most striking I have seen. His presence commanded attention. He was an excellent speaker, one of the best I have ever heard. He was a leader of men and he usually got what he wanted.

He had been educated in Denmark and was strongly influenced by the folk school movement. Like Caesar, he came, he saw, he conquered.

When he arrived at Nysted, he was not married, and I can imagine that many a Nysted girl had palpitation of the heart when she saw him.

He had not been there long till one farmer was telling the other that the new preacher had something to say and

Pastor and Mrs. Thorvald Knudsen

knew how to say it. On each Sunday there were fewer and fewer vacant pews in the church.

One Sunday after church, he announced that at eight o'clock next Friday evening he would start reading a novel for the young people. This was the beginning of the Young People's Society. Four of my older brothers and sisters walked to Nysted for the reading. He read **Ben Hur** by Wallace in a Danish translation. He was an excellent reader and more and more young people came to listen. My brothers and sisters came home with great enthusiasm. I was sorry that I could not join the fun.

Not long after, Pastor Knudsen announced that he would teach the young people Danish gymnastics. They came faithfully and it was not long till their steps were lighter and they held their heads a little higher.

For boys under twelve, he organized a rifle club. Under his supervision, we met every Sunday afternoon for practice. All farmers wanted their boys to learn how to use guns, so this was a popular movement. How proud a boy was when he hit the bull's-eye and won a word of praise from the pastor.

Things were really happening in Nysted, and more was to come. The pastor called a meeting at which the condition of the buildings and grounds was discussed. It was now some months since Pastor Strandskov had left and much had been neglected. Soon a large group of farmers was working under Knudsen's direction; men, women and young people all working and having a lot of fun. A lawn was seeded, flowers and shrubs were planted and a system of irrigation was installed. Nysted could now boast a fountain with sparkling and laughing waters. In the course of a year or so, the place was a beauty spot on the Nebraska prairies.

The folk school was remodelled and an addition was added. It became more attractive and the attendance increased.

Pastor Knudsen had not been there more than a year or two, when he told the people that he was making a quick journey to Denmark. He did not say publicly what was the purpose of his errand, but soon enough it was known that he was to be married there.

When the people knew what date he was returning to Nysted, there was feverish activity. Everything had to be spick-and-span for the young bridal couple. A triumphal arch was built in their honor. It was not quite as elaborate as the one in Paris, but these people had not been in Paris and they were surely impressed. There would be a fine banquet to welcome them.

Long before it was time for the pastor and his wife to arrive, the people began to gather in Nysted. They wanted to be sure that all was in readiness. It was. When their buggy was seen coming over the hill east of Nysted, the people, old and young, lined up on both sides of the road. As they came into the village, the people sang a song of welcome. This was written by one of the local poets for the occasion. Pastor Knudsen and his wife, Thora, stepped from the buggy. I heard many a woman say, "Isn't she beautiful." She was.

They were led to a banquet hall and here the festive board was covered with good food. After the eating, there was much speaking and singing with Skoal, Skoal. There could have been no doubt in the minds of the Knudsens that they were welcome.

It was my good fortune to be old enough to go to Pastor Knudsen for instruction for confirmation. We went twice a week for about two hours each time. This was Wednesday afternoon and Saturday morning. He told us the stories of the Bible as I have not heard them told before or since. In my mind I could see Adam and Eve walking through the shaded lanes of Paradise. I was there when God visited Abraham and Sarah. I was filled with fear when Abraham was about to offer his son, and relieved when he was told to take the tangled ram in place of his boy. I was not the only one who sat as in a trance. The attention of us children was perfect, and he demanded it. Woe unto the boy or girl whose attention strayed!

About the only preparation we had for Pastor Knudsen was that we had to learn certain hymns by heart. They were the great Danish hymns of Grundtvig, Brorsen, Kingo and Ingeman. I know that it was difficult for some of the boys and girls, but I am glad that it was demanded of me. It is now scores of years since I learned these hymns, and many of those great poems are still with me.

One day Knudsen was called from the class. He returned after about ten minutes. I could see that he had learned something that had shocked him. He told us that a former pupil of his, Hans Enevoldsen, had committed suicide in Wyoming. As I recall it now, this was the first suicide of which I heard.

Confirmation day was a great day for us. We were all in new clothes and most self-conscious. When the time came, we boys and girls stepped up to the altar and Pastor Knudsen talked to us. We all felt that he liked us. He talked to us about King David. I doubt that any of that class of fourteen has ever forgotten it.

Many years later I met a man who had been in that class. I asked him if he still remembered Pastor Knudsen. With a light in his face, he replied, "That is the best and greatest man I have ever known." He surely expressed the sentiment of many.

One of the important events of my childhood was the wedding of my oldest sister, Anna. She married a young man, Julius Jensen, who had worked for father in 1893. He had bought an eighty-acre farm about a half mile from our home. Weddings in those days were big affairs. Father and mother, together with the betrothed, made the plans, and father consulted with Pastor Knudsen about every detail. It was important to have his approval. When the number of guests had been reduced to the absolute minimum, it was found that there would be about two hundred people present. Obviously, such an affair could not be held at home. It would have to be at Nysted where there was a hall large enough to accomodate the crowd.

For some weeks, our house was a beehive of activity. A woman was brought in to help with the sewing. Mother and the girls were busy with a hundred things such as planning the food for the celebration. Father arranged for the dance orchestra, and Julius Jensen made arrangements to have the local band there. He had played the drum in the band for some time.

Throughout the community, the coming wedding was a chief topic of conversation and planning. In order that each family should not bring some little gift, it was the practice for some interested party to canvass all invited guests and ask them how much each wanted to contribute to the "present fund." When the money had been collected, a committee went to town and bought what it thought best. Furniture, hardware and silverware were among the things usually bought.

The great day came and everything was ready. Shortly after noon we all drove to Nysted, where all the relatives gathered at the home of the groom's parents, Mr. and Mrs. Kristian Jensen. He was the manager of the local savings bank. Before three o'clock, the members of the band came, tuned their instruments and lined up in march formation. Immediately following the band in the procession came Pastor Knudsen and his wife, followed by the bridal couple, my parents, the groom's parents, bridesmaids, best men and other relatives. We children brought up the rear. The band struck the first notes of a march and slowly and majestically the procession moved toward the church, which was already filled to capacity. It had been decorated beautifully for the festival. Seats were reserved for the bridal retinue. We children found room where we could. Pastor Knudsen now took charge. First the people sang a couple of hymns, after which the pastor stepped to the altar and beckoned to the couple to come forward. There was my sister, the center of attraction. She was beautiful as she stood there in her light grey dress with a spray of myrtle in her hair and the bridal veil extending from her head to the floor. The groom, too, was handsome in his dark suit. I liked him especially because he had given me so many rides on his bicycle, and had even let me try to ride it by myself.

The ceremony was simple. There was no giving the bride away, or ring ceremony. The pastor gave a short talk, which today would be called a sermon. After the mutual promises had been made, the congregation sang another hymn or two, and the people left the church led by the bride and groom.

While the people stood about visiting, father saw to

it that cigars were passed around and the band played several numbers. I was enjoying all of this and I was hoping that my brother, Chris, would not see me, but he did and very soon came with the depressing information that it was time for us to go home and do the chores.

We walked home. I was in bad spirits. But cows and pigs do not celebrate human marriages and must eat regardless of human institutions. How we rushed through the chores. Even the pigs were surprised. Rural tradition holds that the last milk that a cow gives contains the cream. If that is true, I am sure that we got little cream that afternoon. We were back in Nysted before the wedding dinner. Other young people were also flocking to the village and there was a large crowd by now.

At the appointed hour, the master of ceremonies shouted that dinner was served, and asked the older people to take places first. Of course the children had to wait. But this was one time when we children did not have to wait. At this wedding we were important. It was our sister who was being married. What was more, we were given places of honor at the table, not so far from the bridal couple. I could hardly believe the bride was my sister. She looked so distinguished. I was wondering if she knew me anymore.

Pastor Knudsen was the toastmaster and took charge. He said grace and told the people that it was now time to be happy and enjoy the food. The eating began and it was plainly seen that appetites were good, but this was not an ordinary farm meal. It was much more formal. Every one used his best manners, which in an uncouth age were not any too good. When the meal was well advanced, Pastor Knudsen rose and proposed a toast to the newly-wedded. The people raised their wine glasses and there was many a Skoal, Skoal. There were speeches and more Skoals. A song had been written for the occasion and this was sung with high spirits.

When all adults had been served, the children had their meal. While they were eating, cigars were passed around again, and the band played. It takes time to feed a couple of hundred hungry people, and it was hard work for the waiters and the women who worked in the kitchen.

Once the dinner was over, the young men began to clear the floor of the tables and benches and make ready for the dance. The floor was swept and wax was applied freely.

Meantime the orchestra, consisting of three members, had arrived. There was the fiddler, the flute player and the organist. After a protracted period, of what seemed to me useless tuning, they were ready and a nod was given to the master of ceremonies.

He took his place and announced that the first dance would be a waltz for the bridal couple. The orchestra struck the note and sweet music filled the hall, and my sister and her husband stepped forward and began to dance. They danced well, for they had spent many a pleasant hour doing that. While they danced round and round the hall all alone, the people stood back in awed silence.

The announcer now said that the next dance would be a waltz for the bridal couple, the bridesmaids and the best men. These couples now danced. It was a progressive affair. In the next waltz, the parents of the bridal couple were included, and in the following the young men and women who had waited tables took their turn on the floor.

Finally the announcer cried, "Everybody waltz." And waltz they did; old people and young together with children mingled among them in one grand harmony of old-fashioned swing. In an atmosphere of sweat, cigar smoke, and dust they danced. They danced with vigor and joy, laughing and talking. There was no cold war or a threat of a hot one. They knew nothing about atoms and hydrogen bombs. They danced waltzes, two-steps and polkas. Then there was a number of Danish group dances.

Between dances the men would go outside for a few puffs of smoke and the women used their fans diligently. While the floor was clear, the children came forward in swarms to slide. The floor was so slick that it was not easy to maintain a balance, and many of them rolled and caused others to fall.

The dancing went on till about midnight when the tables and benches were set up again. This time for a lunch. Everybody had coffee, cake and sandwiches. It was almost a second dinner. The play had been hard and appetites were good.

When the tables and benches had been cleared again, the dancing went on. The oldest and the youngest, by this time, were showing signs of fatigue. The former went home and the latter fell asleep. They lay on tables, chairs and in corners. The platform where the orchestra sat, was littered with sleeping bits of humanity. That they could sleep in all the noise and dust was surely of sign of excellent nerves.

At about two o'clock the master of ceremonies announced that there would be a pause for coffee punch. There was talk that Pastor Knudsen did not like these drinking songs. At any rate, he and his wife left before this time. Coffee punch was a mixture of rum and coffee. Large bowls of the beverage were set forth and each adult filled his cup. With the bridal couple in the center, the people drank and sang. There was a Danish drinking song which was always used for this happy occasion. With many a Skoal, Skoal and long live the bride and the groom, they drank.

After this pause the dancing was resumed. My sister had not missed a dance all night. Everybody who could must dance with her. How proud I was as I waltzed with the bride.

One of the crowning events at these weddings was a solo dance by one of the farmers. He was an odd person, who during his daily grind on the farm, was inclined to be morose. But at a wedding, with a liberal supply of coffee punch to cheer body and soul, he was certainly not morose. It usually took some coaxing on the part of the master of ceremonies, but he always came forward finally. Following the announcement that Mads Rasmussen would now do the "Syv Spring," he stepped to the middle of the floor. There was a round of applause, and he began his labor of love. It was a complicated dance, and as it progressed, he became more and more graceful. Back and forth he moved with the greatest of ease. He tip-toed. He whirled and whirled. It made me dizzy just to look at it. The dance ended with a low bow, to the very floor. Amidst a storm of applause he arose and retired.

In the meantime dawn was beginning to touch the eastern skies and in the stillness of the night one could hear the rattle of wagons and buggies carrying tired but happy people home from the wedding dance. When we came home, it was almost daylight. After we had unhitched the horses from the buggy, father said we would do the chores before retiring. We children did them half asleep, and then to bed.

The crossroads store in the nineties was an interesting institution. The one at Nysted was a social center as well as a store. One could go there for groceries, jeans and news. It was open from eight in the morning till ten at night except Sunday when it was open for some time in the morning.

When one entered the store there were groceries, etc., on the right and yard goods, notions, etc., on the left. In the grocery department there were no "Hidden Persuaders." The few packaged things had neither sex nor eye appeal. In packages I recall soap, corn starch, gloss starch, Arbuckles and Lions coffee. In canned goods there were salmon and sardines. Most of the groceries one bought in bulk and were contained in boxes, barrels and drawers. The clerk put such things into paper sacks: sugar, rice, sago, oatmeal, corn meal, raisins, prunes, dried apples, dried peaches, crackers and cookies. On the shelves, too were found different brands of smoking tobacco. This was usually contained in cotton bags, and one early brand was Bull Durham. On a shelf there was also a place for chewing tobacco and a knife for slicing off a plug of tobacco. A popular brand was "Horseshoe." There were no cigarettes for sale. They were called coffin nails and were considered bad for both body and soul. There were a few brands of cigars in boxes. On a counter stood a box containing smoking tobacco. This was for the customers. One was welcome to fill his pipe from this box without cost. There were also free matches. One was expected to use moderation in using free tobacco and matches.

On a counter was a large round cheese. It was always covered with a wire netting to keep away flies, mice and men. On another counter was a case containing mixed candy and candy bars. When a customer bought a small order, he was given a small bag of candy and when he bought a large one he was given a large bag.

In the aisle stood boxes and barrels. In the boxes could be dried fish and cans of molasses. There was usually a barrel of apples. This, too, was covered with a wire netting. It was not right to tempt the young.

On the left hand side of the store were such things as yard goods, needles, thread, yarn, ribbons, work gloves, overalls, jeans and neckties.

Toward the back of the store and to the right was the post office. Near here and in the right wall was a door that lead to the house of the owner.

Way in the back of the store one could buy such things as coal oil, nails, wire and staples. On the shelves here were lamps and lanterns and also lamp and lantern chimneys.

The owner of the Nysted general store was Ludwig Petersen. He and his good wife, Katrine, managed the place. She did most of the physical work and he furnished most of the brains. He was a man with a history.

They had married and gone west. There he had worked hard and they had prospered. Suddenly a terrible disease struck him. It was painful and devastating. He lost the use of nearly every joint of his body. It was evidently arteriosclerosis. After the disease had run its course, the brave couple moved to Nysted and bought the only store. For some years he was also the postmaster.

Mr. Petersen was a man with a keen mind. He was one of the best read men in the community. He was an expert chess player, and played by mail with some of the keen players of the land.

Mr. Petersen had been a tall man before he was stricken. Now he sat in a wheel chair. He had a lean, intelligent face with dark, deeply set eyes. His hair was black and straight and was combed to the one side. When he leaned forward, the locks fell down his forehead. He threw them back with a quick jerk of his head. Since he could not shave himself and it would have been difficult for another person to do so, he wore a beard. This too was dark. He could not walk and did not wear shoes. Maybe his feet were too crippled for shoes. At any rate, his wife knitted hose for his feet. His hands I shall not forget. They had surely been lean, handsome and strong. Now they were gnarled, twisted and the fingers were drawn up like an eagle's claw grasping something, though the finger nails had been ruined by the terrible disease. He could not move a finger, but once he had a pen wedged between two crooked fingers on his right hand, he wrote beautifully. He surely had the best handwriting in the community. He also did fine pen drawings, and there must be a good many of them among his relatives.

It seemed that about the only joints he could use with any ease, were those of his neck and back. He could talk, but he could not feed himself. His wife did that. He loved a good cigar. His wife put it on a stick and lit it for him and then he managed it somehow with his disabled hand. He had a hearty laugh and when laughing, his emaciated body shook strongly. How his wife managed to get him in and out of bed, I do not know. They did have four children.

In time they worked up a fair business. They were thrifty and won a circle of friends.

At about the turn of the century, Mr. Petersen went through a spiritual crisis. The cruel mockery of his life was becoming too much. He was losing his will to live, and became indifferent to his family, his friends and his business.

Up to this time, he had not taken much interest in the village church. He was considered a bit hostile to it.

However, when Pastor Knudsen heard of Petersen's illness, he knew that here would surely be a great challenge to him. He spent hours and finally days with the sick man. There were long discussions, sharp debate and quiet conversations. Peace came back to his tortured soul. Pastor Knudsen told my father later that it was the most strenuous piece of work that he had ever done. After the Knudsens had left Nysted, I chanced to be talking to Mr. Petersen about him and he remarked to me, "With the exception of my wife, I owe that man more than any other person."

Once again, Mr. Petersen took his place in the community and entered into all its phases more completely. He had a good sense of humor. Those who played cards with him, said it was most fun. Strange is it not that this cripple should be the one who often brought cheer to many a man whose body was whole.

I had one experience with Mr. Petersen that I shall not forget. One noon my friend, Harry Hansen, and I walked to the village store. My parents had asked me to get something there. On our way, we conceived a mighty slick plan; we had no money, but we would get candy anyway. Since talking was easy for me and I spoke Danish well and Harry did not, I was to occupy the attention of Mr. Petersen while Harry helped himself to the delicious candy. When we entered the store, with a deep sense of guilt, we saw that Mr. Petersen was sitting in his wheel chair by his post office desk. I walked up to him with pretended courage. I tried to say something clever. It was stupid. Then I tried to be nonchalant, but he saw immediately what a fool I was. My act was a total flop. With his elbow he wheeled his chair back where he could see Harry. He called to him that he should bring the stolen goods up to his desk. He did that. There lay the candy, and there we stood in the presence of a cripple who was far more clever than we. He did not say much to us. His silence was eloquent. As my friend and I walked back toward school, I hated myself and wondered what would happen to me when Mr. Petersen told father. He never did. From that time on, I loved him more.

X

MORE WORK AND PLAY

Long before the end of the century all the land in Howard County was occupied. The Danes had established several other settlements such as at Dannevirke and Cushing. There were several thousand Danes in the county.

Our part of the county was pretty much a cross section of America. The Danes occupied the land on both sides of Oak Creek from its mouth to about twelve miles north and west. To the east and north were Yankees and Canadians, to the north were Poles, to the west were Germans and to the south were Swedes. In the beginning these nations lived pretty much apart. As time went on, there was more and more blending.

For many years the village of Dannebrog had a big celebration on June 5th. June 5th is Denmark's constitution day. On that day Danes, Yankees, Swedes, Poles and Germans celebrated together.

In our home June 5th was, of course, celebrated. For several years Chris and I were allowed to walk to Dannebrog as soon as we had completed the morning chores. Father had given each of us a quarter and by the time we had reached town, our plans were complete as to how the money was to be spent. There would be a nickel for a carousel ride, a nickel for firecrackers, a nickel for peanuts, a nickel for candy and one nickel was kept in reserve for some unknown contingency.

Presently we were joined by other boys from our neighborhood, and we made a survey of what there was to see and there was much for mentally hungry boys. We watched in open-eyed wonder at any stunt.

One of the first things we did was to have a ride on the carousel. This heavenly thing was owned by a German farmer whose name was Mr. Reimer. His machine was small, simple and primitive. It was hand-pushed. Mr. Reimer had a place of honor on his carousel. He stood and cranked the hand organ, while his boys pushed the merry-go-round. They went to the celebrations in all the towns in the county. How I envied his boys. Here they were going round and round listening to sweet organ music, while I was down on the farm, barefooted and wearing homemade jeans, listening to the mooing of cows and the grunting of pigs. There was no justice!

One year disaster struck. Mr. Reimer had set up his carousel and was waiting for business, when a steam-driven one came to town and was set up next to his. The new one had a fine whistle and was gaudily decorated, and the horses actually loped as it went round and round. People flocked to the new carousel and Mr. Reimer and his machine were neglected. He cut prices, but to no avail. He and the boys sat and watched the multitude. I doubt that he would agree with Shakespeare when he said that the uses of adversity are sweet.

At an appointed time, Chris and I were to meet the rest of the family at some designated place. They brought the lunch and by that time we were starved. As soon as they arrived, the team was unhitched and tied to the buggy and given a feed. There were hundreds of teams standing in open spaces in town. Mother spread a table cloth on the grass and we ate our lunch. Chris and I told them about the wonders we had seen. Father asked us how much money we had spent and urged us to use it wisely. There would be no more for us that day. He meant it.

The town was decorated in its best. There were American and Danish flags all over. By two o'clock, there were hundreds of people in the village. During my boyhood there were several Danish signs on business places. Where medicine was sold, there was dignity and quiet. One could buy pills but not cosmetics and lawn mowers. It was not called a drug store, but over the door was the sign **Apotek**.

Hundreds of farm women came to town too. I am sure that most of them needed this little diversion. Many communities had so little of it. With their many children these women walked back and forth on the hot boardwalks. Many of them looked so drab and so tired. Soon their little children were crying and that added to the burden. In those days, one could hear a half dozen languages in Dannebrog.

Along in the afternoon there was a speaker or two. In the early days, one spoke in the Danish language and one in the American. Since there were many who spoke neither, I don't suppose they got much out of it. The speakers' stand was in a park. While this was not a Tivoli, it was nice. On the edge of the park was the creek. Once during a patriotic speech, a child fell into the water and screamed wildly. All the people rushed off to rescue the child. What the speaker did, I do not know.

There was a cute little steamboat on the creek. It could sail up the creek for about a mile. Mother took some of us children for a ride. It had a whistle and this was truly travelling in style.

One of the most exciting events of the day was a tug of war. During many years, this event was between the Danes and the Germans. Germany was the traditional enemy of Denmark. A call went out for the heaviest and strongest Danes. I was sorry that father was tall and slim and was not in demand as a power. With the heaviest Dane at the end of the rope and other husky Danes ahead of him, they were now ready for the ancient adversary. The signal was given. My heart was in my throat. I knew that God was in His heaven, but if the Germans won, all was not right with the world.

It has been one of the wonderful things about America that these old animosities between the European nations soon looked silly and finally disappeared.

It was at one of these celebrations that I tasted my first ice cream soda. I heard a more sophisticated person order one with strawberry flavor. I didn't know what that was and what it cost. I asked him and he told me. I told the waiter, "I'll take the same." It was wonderful.

There were barkers along the streets who sold all the lemonade (mostly water) you could drink for a nickel. The saloons did a land office business, and many a weary farm wife had to haul a drunk man home. There were small firecrackers and giant firecrackers. One farmer surprised his wife and children by blowing off his hand.

Some time during the early afternoon, there was a parade. The various business firms had floats and scattered little gifts to the crowd. There was a wild scramble for them. One year I caught a small package. In it was a bottle of patent medicine. This was guaranteed to cure the worst case of running bowels. I drank it all at once. I suffered no ill effects.

There were bicycle races. It was a three-mile race, and by some people and animals these speed demons were considered dangerous.

Along in the afternoon there was a band concert in the park. This was welcomed, especially by the women. It seemed that the children were less unruly when the band played.

The ball game came late in the afternoon and was played in a nearby cow pasture. The games were usually between young fellows of neighboring towns. One year we saw Grover Cleveland Alexander from Elba pitch a fine game. Already as a young fellow he had both speed and grace. Later he won national fame as a great pitcher.

Father had told us that we were all to meet at the buggy at five-thirty. We met there promptly, if reluctantly. We wanted so much to have stayed for the evening fireworks, but that was out of the question. There were the usual chores. On the way home, we children did not have much to say. We were tired.

When the chores had been done and we had eaten a little supper, we waited for the fireworks. We could easily see them from our home. It was a grand sight!

It was incredible how much the boys of our neighborhood walked. We walked to school. We walked to Nysted for the mail. We walked behind the plow, cultivator and harrow. We walked to the meetings at Nysted. Horses worked in the fields and their right to rest must be respected. It was not that we always did this walking with enthusiasm. It was a necessity.

On Sunday afternoons the boys of our neighborhood were usually together. There were the brothers Victor and Thomas Hermansen, and their cousins Thomas S. and Harry Hermansen, Edward Jensen, Chris and myself. Some or all of us spent much time together along Oak Creek. We knew the best swimming holes and used them a great deal. It is true that there were turtles, snakes and ticks in the holes, too, but that did not annoy us. One day Tom Hermansen was seized with cramps in the water and went down two times. We pulled him to safety and none was much concerned. We knew where the best wild plums and wild cherries were and ate till we were full.

With the girls we played such games as Throw the Pole, Hide and Go Seek, Clap in Clap Out and Drop the Handkerchief. One game we boys played with much enthusiasm was Foot and a Half. It required considerable skill and was very popular for a while.

One cold winter day, five of us boys decided to skate to Dannebrog. We had no idea how far it was along the meandering Oak Creek. We received the permission of our parents and met at the appointed time: nine o'clock Sunday morning. The ice was fair and we set out with a shout, but it was much farther than we had estimated. It became work. In our eagerness to be off, none of us had thought of carrying a lunch. We became very hungry and tired. We did not reach Dannebrog till two in the afternoon. Starved, we pooled our resources. We had five pennies among us. For these we bought some candy, and slowly walked the long way home. After Chris and I had helped with the chores that night, we need not be told to go to bed. We simply fell in.

I suppose I was about fifteen when father bought a hay and pasture farm. It was about five miles southeast of Dannebrog and about nine miles from home. At about the same time, Martin Hermansen bought a similar farm next to ours. His boys were Thomas S. and Harry, and we had been friends for some time. In the spring we drove the young cattle to pasture. We usually rode a horse for this. About the middle of the summer we boys went over there to put up hay. We stayed there overnight. Father and Mr. Hermansen came in the morning. They brought our lunch. They drove home at night. We boys liked this life very much. We felt grown up and were really "roughing it." We mowed the green grass. One day the sickle of my mower ran into a nest of bumble bees. They attacked me. In panic I ran away from both mower and horses. This was a foolish thing to do, but any person who has had intimate experience with bumblebees, will know why I ran and fought like a madman. The other boys did not feel sorry for me. They laughed and laughed. The bees stung me so many places on my face that I became ill. My face was badly swollen, and the boys said that I was the "spitten image" of William Jennings Bryan.

That year there were so many bumblebees that it was dangerous to work in the hayfield. Something had to be done. A neighbor told us how to destroy the foe. Each worker covered his hands and face. We filled a jug half full of water, went to the nests of the bees, set the jug on the ground, beat the earth and stirred up the bees until they were totally mad. In their fury they swarmed about until they found the jug and into this they flew to certain death.. Peace returned to the meadow.

We four boys slept in a haymow. The only light we had was from a kerosene lantern. It was not good, but it was good enough to read novels by. There in the haymow, we lay around the lantern reading interesting stories. Some of them were written in the Danish and some in the English language. The one I remember most clearly is "Around the World in Eighty Days" by Jules Verne. This was a

103

marvelous story. I saw it all in glory. That story read by lantern light in an old haymow was just as brilliant as the movie I saw of it more than fifty years later.

One season our parents must have felt more prosperous than usual. They decided that they would not carry our lunch over to us, but that we should buy our meals from a Mrs. Hurst who lived not far away. This pleased us greatly. It was a sure sign that we were coming up in the world. The breakfast was just ordinary, but when we boys arrived for the evening dinner, we experienced something new in our young lives. The table was beautifully set, considering rural appointments. There were flowers on the table, and beside the table stood two young, sweet girls. They asked us to be seated. All four of us took our places. Then each girl stepped up to the table and began to use her fan. This was done to keep our faces cool and to keep away pesky flies. The girls were embarrassed and we boys were amazed and amused. We hardly dared to look up. We might burst into laughter. This could happen in a Jules Verne story but not to boys who had to sleep in a haymow! I have travelled in many lands since then, but I have not eaten in such grandeur.

Quite early in the present century father became the shipper of the Nysted Co-operative Shipping Association. About two times a month this organization shipped hogs and/or cattle to the South Omaha market.

On a Saturday father would go to Nysted and there the farmers would come and tell him what they had of cattle or hogs to be shipped the following week. When father had the necessary information, he would be in a position to order the necessary number of railway stock cars. For many years it was my task to ride my pony to Dannebrog to order the cars at the railway station.

On the day set for shipping, in hot summer and in cold winter, father would drive to Dannebrog early in the morning to weigh each load of hogs and cattle. When all the animals had been gathered in the stockyards it was his job to load the cars and to report to the station agent when the loading was done. Very often this association shipped three or four carloads at a time.

Quite often father would travel in the caboose with the livestock train to South Omaha. When a shipper had two cars, he was given a return ticket by the railway company.

Once when I was about seventeen years of age, father let me go with him to Omaha on the stock train. I was in ecstacy. It was my first ride on a train. I had been told that the train travelled so fast that one could not count the passing telegraph poles. I was so disappointed when the freight went so slowly toward Grand Island that I could count the passing fence posts!

We changed cabooses in Grand Island. This was the largest city I had seen and I asked father if Chicago was any larger. Soon we found our South Omaha train on the Union Pacific main line.

Our train left Grand Island at about ten-thirty. By this time I was beginning to feel that I was a young man of the world. Father and I had actually eaten our supper in a restaurant! As soon as our freight train was in motion, I noticed that the caboose ran much more smoothly on this line than on the branch line.

There were so many things to see that there was no time for sleep. During the night we passed through such well-lighted cities as Columbus, Schuyler and Fremont. It was all so exciting.

All through the night father talked endlessly with other stockmen. It was one of the first times that I noticed how thick his foreign accent was, but it did not seem to trouble him at all.

Once or twice during the night when the train stopped, father and I got off the caboose and walked along the train to see if our stock was all right. It was.

Our train arrived in South Omaha about seven-thirty in the morning. We had our breakfast and went to the office of the commission firm to whom the stock had been consigned. We were told that all of our animals were in good shape and that they had been carefully watered and fed.

When the buyers from the packing houses came to buy the stock, father and I went out to watch them. To me these buyers were most impressive in their smart clothes, high boots and each carrying a riding whip. They were often on horseback and it was wonderful to see their horses move about with grace and speed.

It was, of course, the work of the commission men to sell the stock to the buyers. Father was happy when the market was good.

When our stock had been sold, we went back to the Exchange building. There I saw the stock buyers enter with their dirty boots. One of the first things they did was to go to a shoe shining parlor and have their boots cleaned and shined.

The commission firm gave us our dinner and simple age that it was, one of the men asked us to spend the night in his home.

In the afternoon father and I saw some of the sights. We went through one of the packing houses and saw them killing hogs. It was a bloody mess, but I had not yet read **The Jungle** by Upton Sinclair. I had not seen a streetcar before and I had not seen electric lights. In Omaha I saw electric signs that flickered brilliantly during the night. Up to this time, I had not seen a building over three stories high. Here I saw buildings with fifteen stories. We took an elevator to the top of this building. What a thrill!

When evening came, I was dead tired. I had not slept the night before. But tired as I was, I was awakened quite often by strange noises. A streetcar went past the house where I slept. We had no such noise at home. Some blocks away were the railway yards with whistles on the Union Pacific and Burlington trains. They, too, woke me up.

Next morning father and I took a passenger train to Grand Island. I was by now too tired to stay awake. We changed trains in Grand Island and St. Paul. One of the boys met us at the station in Dannebrog. I had been out in the wide, wide world. While I had not been in Iowa, I had looked across the Missouri River and into Iowa.

When the report of the stock sale reached father by mail, it was his job to figure how much each farmer would receive for the animals he had sold. It was not a simple problem. We boys helped and I made my share of mistakes. But finally we did find the right answers and father left the account at the local bank where each farmer got his money. If he had any doubts about the accuracy of the amount, he could examine the papers. They were right there.

Father's great strength was his ability to get along with people. He heartily disliked strife. He was an expert at pouring oil on troubled waters.

Some time about 1905 a family by the name of Feddersen moved into our community. Mr. Feddersen and father soon became good friends.

In the course of time Mr. Feddersen rented a farm from Peter Krogh of Farwell. All of the terms are not known to me now, but each did own one-half of all the cattle and pigs.

Mr. Feddersen and Mr. Krogh were surely honorable men, but for some reason they just could not get along with each other. Perhaps both men were too easy to anger. Soon it was heard that a lawsuit was coming up. Father was deeply disturbed when he heard the news. Both men belonged to our church and he was sure that both men would lose by such a suit. Since he knew Mr. Feddersen better than Mr. Krogh, he went and talked with him and got his side of the story. Then he drove to Farwell and talked to one of Mr. Krogh's good friends. This man went and had a long talk with Mr. Krogh. In the end it was so arranged that the two adversaries agreed to a plan of mediation. Father represented Mr. Feddersen and the other man represented Mr. Krogh, and these two men chose a third who was J. Jensen, a respected merchant from Dannebrog. Krogh and Feddersen had agreed to abide by the decisions of these three men, and a day was set for the division of the things on the farm.

Father took me along to the Krogh farm which Feddersen had rented. All day long I chased pigs, cows and calves. These animals were divided into lots and every other time Feddersen or Krogh had the first choice. When evening came the things had been divided to the general satisfaction of both parties. At the end of a long day, Feddersen and Krogh shook hands. The three men who had helped to settle their deep grievances peacefully went home happy, though they had received not a penny for their good work.

XI

SUNSET AND EVENING STAR

The Lord's my shepherd, I'll not want;
He makes me down to lie
In pastures green, He leadeth me
The quiet waters by.

During all these years, mother's health had been good. She had given birth to eight children, and had worked very hard. She could soon begin to take it a bit more easy. However, after the birth of my youngest brother, Holger, she did not seem so well. One day early in the new century, she was doing some work in her dear garden. Suddenly, there was a sharp pain in her lower abdomen. To begin with, we were not very much concerned. The pain increased during the night, and a doctor was called from Dannebrog. He diagnosed it as a temporary case of an upset stomach. He gave her some medicine, but during the night she became worse. We called the doctor again. He now saw that this was serious, and said that he would like to call in a doctor from St. Paul. This was Dr. Grothan. He came and said that it was an intestinal obstruction, and that surgery would be necessary and at once. Our living room was converted into an operating room. The dining room table was used for an operating table. It became dark and there by the light of a kerosene lamp, mother was given chloroform and an operation was performed. My father held the lamp and my oldest sister was the nurse. Dr. Grothan called the operation a success and said that if it had been delayed a few hours, gangrene would have set in and the disease would have been fatal. She recovered.

A teacher in the local public school had persuaded father that a small business college in St. Paul would be the place to further my education. I went there for three months, and as I look back at the educational experience, if it may be called that, I can't help wondering if most of the faculty had ever mentally ventured outside of Howard County. The only course I took which was taught with any imagination and skill was a course in Roman history.

Before I left, I had to promise mother that I would keep in close touch with her. She seemed so concerned about me and was not very cheerful that winter.

During the following winter, my two brothers were away and I did the farm work. When I was confirmed I was the smallest boy in the class. I was now six feet tall and it seemed that my bones hung together very loosely and I was very self-conscious.

When a carload of coal for the folk school arrived in Dannebrog, friends of the school hauled the coal free. Father told me to haul a load. I drove to town, loaded my wagon from a railway car and set out for Nysted where I arrived at about five o'clock. Another load was being unloaded ahead of mine and I had to wait. Students not in class were running around and there was quite a bit of excitement which made the horses nervous. When it was my time to drive up and unload, one of my horses balked. It reared and jumped, but would not pull. I had an audience and was mortified almost beyond endurance. The students roared with laughter. My brother, Chris, who was attending the school, came and took charge. He was better at handling horses than I, and soon the horses were under control and pulled the load.

I was growing out of my clothes and begged mother for a new suit of Sunday clothes. If one of us could convince her, she could usually convince father. One day in the barn, father said to me. "Your mother is not well. I wish you would not annoy her about clothes for yourself." I was ashamed of myself. I knew that mother had not looked well, but I had been too self-centered to give it much thought.

From time to time, she went to see the local doctor, but there was no great change either way.

Christmas came and on Christmas Eve we were all at home. My oldest sister and her family were there. It was so nice that we were all at home again. We listened to the Christmas chimes as usual, and had been asked to take our places at the table for the Christmas dinner. Father had said grace and we were just beginning to eat, when mother became sick and had to leave the table. With her left the happy Christmas spirit. She stayed close to home during the holidays.

Dr. Grothan was called again. He told us that some exploratory surgery would be necessary. This, too, was done at home. My brothers and I walked around in a daze, waiting and waiting. After a while, my sister, Marie, came out to us. She was crying. This was an ominous sign. The doctor left. Father told us that mother's disease was of a fatally malignant kind and that nothing could be done. The darkness deepened.

For some weeks she lingered. She was beautiful in her patience, even when the pain was severe. She was sorry to die and said so. We children were nearly everything to her, and she wanted so much to see all of us grow to maturity. However, she did not seem to fear death. To her death was not the final victor. She professed much and believed all she professed. She died with a prayer on her lips.

110

On a bleak March day we laid her frail body to rest in the good Nebraska earth. She had loved it so. I am sure it received her hospitably.

When we came home, the house, the furniture and the other things were all there, but the house seemed so empty. Something had gone out of it and that something was never restored. Mother was an obscure, simple farm woman, but not too simple to make these words a living truth: **Charity seeketh not her own.**

The best lessons in the love of country I have learned from mother. She was no sunshine patriot. She dearly loved America in good times and bad. It gave her the security of a home. She was deeply thankful that we children did not have to leave home as early as she did. She rarely left her American home for any length of time. She was out of the state only once between 1879 and 1908. She and father attended a church meeting at Tyler, Minnesota in 1905. When she saw the wooded area around Mankato, she said it reminded her of her beautiful birthplace.

What she knew of Danish culture, she loved. It gave her something to live by. Father visited Denmark once while she lived. But she did not care to go back. She said they were so poor and poverty is always hard.

Father and mother gave us a feeling of security that I am certain that many modern children lack. I felt our home stood on a solid rock. We children were often angry and disappointed, but in our heart of hearts, we knew that our parents loved us. We all knew we were wanted.

The old farm home did not break up. My two sisters, Marie and Agneta, kept it going. For this they deserve much credit. It gave my brother, Holger, the security of a home. Then, too, the girls made a good home for father till he died in 1937.

XII

FOLK SCHOOL DAYS

Full of dreams and high ambitions*
For a future rich and fair,
To pursue the noblest visions
And to win through work and prayer:
This is the very soul of youth
Which has in deathless annals
Written its name in truth.

The above lines are taken from a song that the
preacher-poet Kristian Ostergaard wrote and dedicated to
Nysted Folk School in 1900. It was later translated by J.
C. Aaberg. The year 1900 was perhaps the beginning of the
golden age of the Danish folk school in the United States.

There was a rumor in the Nysted congregation that
Pastor Thorvald Knudsen was becoming restless and was
thinking of moving. There was much concern over this,
as he was well-liked and things in church and school had
gone so well. In the spring of 1903, he announced from the
altar of the church that he was leaving as he had accepted
a call from Tyler, Minnesota. The people were stunned.
They could hardly believe it. But it was true. There was
a big farewell festival for the Knudsens and their two little
children. This was one time when a congregation was not
happy to see its pastor leave.

A Pastor A. Th. Dorf and his wife, Thyra, had taught
at the folk school while Knudsen was the headmaster. They
were a remarkably handsome couple. They both sang
beautifully. He played the violin and she played the piano.
Dorf was perhaps the most brilliant man Nysted ever had.

* See **World of Song,** Grand View College, Des Moines, Iowa.

He had graduated from the University of Copenhagen with honors. He read a dozen languages. He was an outstanding actor and many years later played the leading role on a radio program, heard from coast to coast.

He, too, built an addition to the school. My sister, Marie, and my brother, Anker, attended the folk school while Dorf was the headmaster. But for some reason, things at church and school did not go so well. In 1906 he and his family left for Denmark.

The next pastor of the Nysted church and the headmaster of the folk school was Carl Peter Hoiberg. He too was a graduate of the University of Copenhagen. He was about the same age as Pastor Dorf. Pastor Hoiberg had been a professor of theology in the Grand View Seminary in Des Moines, Iowa. A dispute had arisen between him and the president of the institution. The result was that Hoiberg accepted a call from Nysted.

Pastor C. P. Hoiberg

This man came to mean more to me than most teachers I have had, and strangely enough, I can remember very little about the coming of Pastor Hoiberg, his wife, Hilda, and their two children.

Hoiberg enlarged the folk school. He had the west wing built by Strandskov torn down and a larger one built. A bigger tower was erected. Soon attendance in both church and folk school grew.

During the winter of 1908-09, I attended the folk school. It was, of course, a boarding school, and there were enrolled about fifty young men between the ages of 18 and 25. That

113

winter about a fourth of the students were Danish immigrants. One of the chief reasons why these came was to learn the American language. All the students spoke Danish. However, by this time the boys who were born in this country spoke the American language among themselves. Friends of the school had met the students at the railway stations at Dannebrog and Farwell. Most of the students came from Nebraska. There were, however, a few from neighboring states where there were Danish settlements.

One of the first evenings there was an opening meeting to which friends of the school were invited. This was also the occasion for a pantry shower. People came with sacks, bundles and packages. They piled up these gifts on the kitchen tables. There were sacks of sugar, flour and cartons of canned goods in abundance. There were riches here that the old Vikings never dreamed of. All this must have helped the headmaster keep up his morale and to balance the budget.

Mrs. C. P. Hoiberg

This meeting was the official w e l c o m e to the students and to the people of the community. There was the usual group singing first and then the headmaster gave a talk. Following the meeting, coffee was served in the d i n i n g hall. The ladies brought cakes and cookies for the lunch. Following this the people visited until there was a call for devotions.

At seven o'clock sharp in the morning the first bell rang. It was hard to get up, and often one was pulled out of bed by other fellows. That woke him up. In a trice,

114

his face was washed and his hair combed and he was dressed by the time the bell called for breakfast. There was a mad rush down the stairs. Once in the dining hall quiet was restored, for the headmaster stood at the head of one of the tables. Maybe his wife and children were there too. They were not always there for breakfast, but were there for the other meals. The faculty members ate there too. After a word of grace, the boys began to eat. They were hungry and soon learned to eat with speed as Hoiberg was a fast eater and none liked to be the last.

Following breakfast, there were thirty minutes in which to get the rooms, halls, washroom and the gymnasium cleaned. There was a student committee of two that took care of the halls and washroom. There was cold running water in the washroom. This was quite a luxury. There were no indoor toilets. There was a bathhouse back of the school building, where also the outdoor privies were found. Another committee of two damp mopped the floor of the small gymnasium.

At least once a week the headmaster went on a tour of inspection. He looked into each student room and into the halls and the washroom for cleanliness. This he said was a health measure. He mortified a student committee when he found that the washroom was not clean and quietly set about to clean it properly. He did not scold them. His work said more than words. It was incredible what prestige and respect this man enjoyed among these young people.

Under the direction of Mrs. Hoiberg three girls did the housework. Gerda Damgaard did the cooking. Kirsten Kolhede did the baking and helped with the kitchen work. Sigrid Knudsen cleaned the classrooms, the apartment, the halls downstairs, did the washing and helped do the dishes. These three, wonderful girls did all the work; and work they did from long before sunrise till long after sunset. They did it all with a song. Jens C. Jensen was the hired man about the place. He milked the school cows, fed the pigs and horses, helped with the butchering and did the driving. He was also the master mechanic. He saw that things were kept in running order and that the building was warm. This was not so easy as the furnace was not a good one. He too worked many hours every day and did it with a fine spirit.

There were three teachers in addition to the headmaster. Aage Moller, American-born, taught American history, English and arithmetic. P. B. Ammentorp taught Danish, Danish history and geography. Christian Andersen taught singing, Danish literature and gymnastics. Hoiberg was the pastor of the local church and gave the main lecture each day. In addition to this, he was the business manager as well as the bookkeeper.

At eighty-thirty there were morning devotions. Faculty, staff of workers and all the students attended. We were one large family. First there was a morning hymn, a short prayer and another hymn. Announcements were usually made at this time.

Very early in the session, the student organization was formed. A student council was elected and this body chose an editor for the school paper. It was, of course, the students who contributed essays, verse and tidbits. This paper was read at a student meeting Saturday evening. Young people from the community were often present for this meeting, and they as well as faculty and students got their razzing from its pages.

A piggy bank was also established. Deposits for the bank came from a system of fines. These were defined and adopted by the first student meeting. The student council appointed two students each week to detect crime and collect the fines. There were fines for being late to meals and also, for example, playing a musical instrument during quiet hours. If a student refused to pay his fines or to co-operate with the work of the student organization, he was given a ducking under the pump.

At eight forty-five classwork began. There were three subjects that were required of all students. These were: Hoiberg's lecture, singing and gymnastics. During the first week of school we had an opportunity to shop around. We visited most of the classes, and at the beginning of the second

116

week, we handed in our weekly schedule to the headmaster. It had to contain a certain minimum of hours each week. The classes we had selected, in addition to the required classes, we were asked to follow regularly. These were my classes: English grammar and composition, Danish grammar and composition, arithmetic, U. S. history, singing, gymnastics and Hoiberg's main lecture. In U. S. history, English and arithmetic the American language was used. In the other classes Danish was used. The class in U. S. history was a series of lectures. In the other of my classes the traditional method was used.

There was not a student who had graduated from an American high school. The immigrants usually worked harder than the rest of us. They wanted to learn as much English as possible. While there were no credits and no grades given, the students worked about as hard as college students. In English grammar and composition, they were about as advanced or retarded as the average high school graduate today.

Hoiberg's lecture was at eleven o'clock. In addition to the student body, the other teachers attended. Some of the members of the working staff also came if they could find the time. Quite often some people from the village came.

It should be mentioned here that it is the philosophy of the folk school that **what we love is more important than what we know.** I am sure that Hoiberg would agree with that statement. However, I do want to stress that Hoiberg dearly loved knowledge; and his fund of knowledge was prodigious and his ability to memorize was phenomenal. I have known no scholar in any college or university whose mental curiosity in so many fields was so great. If a new element was found in chemistry, he told us boys about it. If a new comet was discovered by some great astronomer, he gave us a lecture about distant stars. When he had an opportunity, he loved to ask us questions about distant lands and peoples. With Socrates he knew that humility is a prerequisite to learning, and he did manage to keep his students humble, in his presence at least.

117

During that winter term he gave us lectures on such topics as Bismarck, Gladstone and Abraham Lincoln. If all the students did not understand the meaning of all the facts, they did understand the spirit of things. Hoiberg was inclined to be idealistic. Too many things were black or white. I suppose his Lincoln and his Gladstone were too white and his Bismarck was too black.

Most of us boys were simple farm boys who had seen almost nothing of the world and knew less. We had not yet learned to be cynical. Some of us worshipped Hoiberg. He could do no wrong. We did not know that human feet are always made of clay. Hitler and Stalin had not done their work. But to this day, I think it was a good experience

Nysted Folk School, 1910

for me. I loved it, and it stimulated me as nothing else had done. Let me mention that I saw Hoiberg in Denmark in 1953. He was eighty years of age, and it was six months before his death. He was learning the Russian language!

We had an hour of singing. This was not choir practice. It was simply group singing, and most students loved to sing. We used a Danish song book published in the United

118

States. Many of the songs were written in this country by Danish-American poets, but most of the songs were written by Danish poets. The songs in this book were grouped under the following headings: Morning Songs, Evening Songs, Christmas Songs, The Christian and Human Life, Nature and Man, Daily Life and Work, Home and Child Life, Youth and Play, Danes in America, Denmark and the Danish people, The School and Enlightenment, Songs About Song, Danish History, Bible History, World and Church History. There is an old saying in the Danish to the effect that the light and serious go well together. They certainly did in that book, and what a range of choices there was. Many of us knew about two hundred of these songs. The school and the Nysted community were singing communities.

The students had physical exercises each school day, and this was no haphazard program, but systematic exercises designed to give exercise to all the important muscles of the body. The exercises were strenuous and the boys got up a good sweat. Then there was tumbling on the mat, which the skillful liked very much. The best gymnasts were often the immigrants.

Before the school term closed, there was a public exhibition. The people of the community liked gymnastics. Many of them had been members of athletic clubs in Denmark, and Nysted had had a gymnastics club for some years. There was a strong applause when something was done well.

The school had no program of organized athletics. Some of the immigrants had played soccer football in Denmark, and we frequently played it on Saturdays and Sundays.

At three in the afternoon we had a coffee break.

There were no classes after five in the afternoon, and at six we had supper. The meals were simple, but there was enough. Most of us gained in weight while we were there.

It would seem that Hoiberg had enough to do, but that winter he found time to read aloud in the evening for all students who cared to listen. Most of them came. He read

119

things in at least three languages, and spoke the English well. It was English rather than American. However, the books he read to us were Danish. He read the great peasant stories written by the Norwegian author, Björnstjerne Björnson. To many of us, these stories were most interesting and charming. Now I do not mean to say that all the students listened eagerly all the time. They did not. Some tired soul slept through each reading.

One evening a week, usually Thursday, the people from the community came to the school. Often there was group singing. The teacher, Christian Andersen, had organized a string orchestra in which he and some students played. They played some good things, mostly from Schumann and Mozart. On some evenings, the students would present a one-act play. On other evenings, Hoiberg or one of the teachers spoke or read something. The attendance was good if the weather was not bad.

It has been mentioned frequently, that the people of the community visited the school and became acquainted with the students. But the students also visited the farm homes. Many of the students later married girls from Nysted. But no farm home was large enough to accomodate fifty-sixty people, so two or three homes sent invitations for the same evening, and let the school divide the school family so that each home had about the same number of guests. The students always walked. They played all kinds of parlor games till a good lunch was served, and what a lunch that was. The hostess could not complain that the students did not like her food. Following that, the students set out for Nysted, often singing most of the way. They were young and life was sweet.

Toward the end of the term, the students gave a piggy bank party and to this the Young People's Society was invited. The fines which had been collected during the term paid for this party, and it was held on a Saturday evening. The students put on a skit or two and selected articles from the student paper were read. Some of the young fellows

120

and girls from the community were given attention also in the paper. The laughter was long and loud.

Following the program there was a lunch with coffee and cake, and after that there was a dance in the gymnasium. This, too, closed with brief devotions.

The term for young men usually closed about the first of March. Farm work was calling. On the last Sunday there was a closing meeting. There were many guests present. There was an exhibition of gymnastics, and there was group singing. Coffee was served and enough chairs and tables were set so that all guests, students and faculty could be seated. There was a toastmaster and students, faculty and farmers gave talks. There was much singing. After that there was a period of devotions and then Good-bye, Good-bye!

Most of the students spent much of the night packing trunks and suitcases. There was much noise and little sleep that night.

Next morning farm wagons came to haul the students to the trains. There were more good-byes. There might even be a few tears. This had been a good life. Maybe it was too good to last.

XIII

TWO FESTIVALS

There were two important festivals each year in Nysted. One was called the March Conference. This came after the students had left, and there had been time to clean up the church and school. Friends of both helped with the work.

The March Conference was really a short folk school stay for people past the usual age for folk school attendance. The guests lived at the school, and the Conference lasted for a week or ten days. Pastors, all Danes, were asked to come and speak. Most of them spoke on religious subjects, but historical and literary subjects were also used.

Very often there were guests from Omaha, Brush, Colorado, and other places where there were Danish congregations. Nysted was a good place to spend a vacation, mixed with learning and inspiration. Many married couples came. For some years, a regular guest was Jorgen Juhl. He was a peddler, a most unusual one. He sold books, lace and notions. His real interests were of the mind and spirit. When he entered a Danish home, the first thing he asked for was the latest church paper. Rumor had it that he had wanted to preach the Gospel, but a speech handicap had prevented that. He had customers in Danish settlements all over the middle west. He walked with a heavy pack on his back all the way from Askov, Minnesota, to Dannevang, Texas; and from Brush, Colorado, to Dwight, Illinois. He told me once that in his travels from Texas to Minnesota, he could stay with friends at night free, nearly all the way. He died in California. A car hit him.

Pastor Hoiberg used to say that when he saw Jorgen

Juhl come up the sidewalk he knew that the meeting had begun.

There were usually forty or fifty guests at the Conference. They sang, they played, they discussed and worshipped together. Some of these people came year after year. There were also meetings in the evenings, and to these the people of the community were invited. Here, too, there were lectures, readings and discussions. The farmers met the Conference guests at the stations, and when they left, it was again the farmers who saw that they met their trains.

Then there was the September Eighth Festival. As mentioned earlier, this was begun by Pastor H. C. Strandskov. The Eighth of September was the birthday of N. F. S. Grundtvig, the father of the folk school idea. This, too, was well attended. It usually lasted for two days.

Most of the guests came by train, and it was again the farmers who met these trains at Dannebrog or Farwell. They had been enrolled ahead of time, so that plans could be made to take care of all. However, some people drove with horse and buggy, if rail connections were poor. I have known people who drove from Ord and Lindsay.

These guests stayed in the homes of the members of the Nysted congregation. For us young people it was a lot of fun to have these guests.

It would probably be conservative to say that the average number of guests early in this century was about one hundred. Some of the more faithful were the Graabecks and Knudsens from Omaha; the Thomsens, the Williamsons, the Rasmussens, the Hansens and the Larsens from Marquette; the Fogeds and the Jensens from Cozad and the Gades and the Christensens from Brush, Colorado.

All through my childhood this was a great festival for my folks. There were many speakers. They were usually the pastors from the Nebraska congregations. One year, and it was a very large meeting, my mother came to me and told me that the very tall man standing on the church steps was the preacher-poet, F. L. Grundtvig, from Clinton, Iowa. He was the son of the great Grundtvig. The Danish church to which we belonged produced other preacher-poets who wrote good things in the Danish. These were at some time or other on the programs of the September Festival. We young people attended as many of the meetings as we had time for. There was still farm work to do. One thing we liked was that so many young people also came. Many of them we knew from earlier meetings here or elsewhere. We played many singing games.

XIV

YOUTH WORK

It will be recalled that a young people's society had been organized at Nysted by Pastor Knudsen. Throughout many years it was active. In my time, there were three outstanding presidents of this organization and they were: Hans Jessen, F. Clarey Nielsen and Thomas S. Hermansen.

While Hoiberg was the pastor of the Nysted church, the society must have had about one hundred members. This organization sponsored dances in the gymnasium, put on home talent plays, organized gymnastic clubs, and folk dancing groups in addition to holding regular meetings. Most of these young people took their places in the church on Sunday mornings. Furthermore, it was these young people who did much of the volunteer work at church and school.

The regular meetings of the society were held either in the folk school gymnasium or in the homes of members. The meetings in the gymnasium usually began with some business followed by a program. There were readings, discussions, and more frequently Hoiberg or some faculty member gave a talk. When this part of the meeting was over, coffee was served, and this was often followed with some games.

It was in summer that the meetings were held in the homes. Nobody had houses large enough for all of these people in winter time. On Sunday afternoon, the young began to arrive at one-thirty or two o'clock. The boys very often brought baseball equipment with them and as soon as there were enough present for two teams, they chose sides and soon there was a hot baseball game going. There was much cheering. Most of the girls had favorites among the players.

At three o'clock, the president of the organization would ring a hand bell and the game would come to a stop. This bell meant that the more serious part of the meeting was about to begin. There was still time to wipe the sweat off a hot brow and to wash up a bit. The meeting was held in some shady place. They sang a couple of songs in Danish, and if there was no business, the program would get under way. Most often it was Pastor Hoiberg who spoke. It could be about Helen Keller or Booker T. Washington. The young people followed what he had to say with real interest, but at times with pretended interest. No one would think of such discourtesy as making noise.

One of the big events of each summer was a picnic close to Dannebrog, near the mouth of Oak Creek. Here there was considerable timber for shade, and water for swimming in the Middle Loup River nearby.

The young people did not drive in their own buggies. They drove in hayracks dressed up for a very special occasion. At a meeting of the society, plans had been carefully laid with committees to take care of the different jobs. There was a committee to make the ice cream and one to take care of transportation.

On Saturday evening, in three or four farm homes, the boys were busy getting the hayracks decorated for the outing. A heavy layer of new mown hay was laid in the bottom of the rack, and the sides were decorated with green branches and with Danish and American flags.

Sunday morning early, there was much activity on many farms of the community. The chores had to be done before the young people could go on the picnic. Food baskets were packed and those who lived near the village walked, and those who lived farther away drove and left their horses in the church barns. It had been decided that the procession had to be ready to leave Nysted at ten o'clock, so there would be no interference with the church service which began at ten-thirty.

Soon the decorated hayracks came down the road, and pulling each were two proud teams of fine horses. The horses, too, had their decorations. Small American flags were set in the harness.

Soon the three racks were loaded with chatting, giggling and laughing young people. The excitement of all this made the horses nervous and some of them reared and pranced with impatience. Now they were off! While the children and elders waved, the hayracks were speeding down the road in a cloud of dust. The young had their song books with them. They sang both Danish and American songs. Most of the American-born now spoke the American language among themselves, but not often to their parents.

It had been agreed ahead of time that when they drove through the pretty village of Dannebrog, the hayracks were to line up close behind one another, and that they should sing certain songs. It was a proud sight to see the three decorated hayracks, filled with happy young people all singing, and each rack pulled by four splendid horses. There had long been some rivalry between these two communities and the Nysted people liked to impress the people of Dannebrog who cheered these young people heartily.

The picnic grounds were about a mile from the village and were in a cow pasture, but these young people were used to cows and bulls. They found a suitable place and began to unload. The horses were unhitched and unharnessed, and tethered to a tree.

The food committee began to make plans for dinner. It was a potluck affair and there was not much preparation, but a fire had to be built so that coffee could be brewed. While this work was being done, other young people explored the area. Some might even try their luck fishing. As always there was a good deal of horseplay, especially by some of the young fellows. This was a perfectly natural thing. They were young and were happy to be with other young people. Then, too, it seems to be an instinct for the boys to show the girls how clever they are.

At about noon, dinner was served. There was an abundance of food. There were no tables. They sat on the grass. It was fantastic the amount of food some of these young people could put away. The farm gave them plenty of exercise and fresh air. Everyone was, or pretended to be, in high spirits.

After the meal there was a period of very little activity. Too much food had been consumed. They strolled around in groups or in pairs. Some of the boys might throw a ball around a bit. Some went boating on the creek.

Some time later one of the boys would shout, "Come on you fellows, let's go swimming." This brought about a good, loud response. The young men went on down to the river by themselves. There was not one swimming suit among them. This was not a mixed beach. Some wore an old pair of pants, and some went into the water as they came into the world, stark naked. The Loup River had a strong current and was deep in places. It had a sand bottom, so the water was clean. It was good swimming and it felt good. Bathing facilities were still very poor in rural homes and what a cleaning these fellows got. There were not many good swimmers among them. About the only method used was the dog paddle, but it was fun. They stayed in the water for at least an hour.

In the meantime, the girls had found another place to swim. Here, too, no one had a swimming suit. Most of them wore old dresses. None could swim so they did not venture into the deep water. But they splashed in the water, got a good cleaning and a good laugh. They stayed in the water about as long as the boys.

By the time that all were dressed and back at the picnic grounds, Pastor Hoibergs had arrived. The young people liked them very much and were glad to see them.

The food committee was now brewing coffee and making ice cream. This was done with a hand freezer and it took some time. It was no snap to turn that thing for a long time. The long stay in the water had made them ravenously hungry. The lunch was welcome.

After lunch they might spend some time singing. The preacher was there now and that called for a little more dignity. Following the singing there were games. These continued till it was time to go home. There were chores on Sunday too.

About five o'clock, they were ready to set out. The horses looked fresh enough, but that was not true of the hayracks. The branches so green in the morning, were now wilted, and the young people were more subdued. There was less singing. They were too tired. The party broke up at Nysted, and each left for his farm home.

The crowning event of each year of the young people's work, was the annual convention. Each church had a society and these were united into districts. Often the districts followed state lines. There was a national organization which was called Danish United Youth whose motto was:
* Steel in your blood,
Fire in your soul
Faith in God.
The Nebraska district did not follow state lines since there were three societies not in the state. There were societies at these places: Nysted, Marquette, Lindsay, Cozad, Cordova, Davey, Kimballton, Iowa; Denmark, Kansas; and Brush, Colorado. The annual convention was held at one of these places. A society knew a year ahead that it would have the convention, and preparations were made.

* See article by Pastor Enok Mortensen in Lutheran Tidings, January 20, 1962

128

There was considerable preparation for such a convention. Delegates were selected. For many years there was a gymnastics tournament. It was usually the men who competed here. For weeks before the convention the young men of a society worked at this. Perfection was the aim. This was true of the setting-up exercises as well as the marching. In the latter, every man must be able to keep step with his team, and be able to make a "to the rear march" without a flaw. In the stunts, on the horse, the bars, or the mat, grace and agility counted. This system of gymnastics had been imported from Denmark, and all the commands were given in the Danish.

Quite often there would be folk dancing groups. These dances were usually Scandinavian in origin. The aim was to do these old dances with the greatest grace. The young people wore ancient costumes for the dance. Usually there were not contests in folk dancing, but often several societies sent dancers.

In fairness it should be said that the Nysted society had some advantages in these exhibitions. Teachers at the folk school often had received special training for such things, and furnished the best leadership in the district.

Some time before the convention, a program had been planned and was published in the young people's paper, "Ungdom," and here was a list of the speakers and other interesting events. This convention lasted two or three days.

Some time before this great event, arrangements had been made on the farms to take care of the work so that as many as possible could go. The younger boys, girls and elders were pressed into service for those days. The young people who were not able to attend such a convention felt neglected.

The young travelled by trains to these meetings. They tried, if possible, to get into the same coach. They were boisterous. They sang both Danish and American songs.

When they arrived at the station there were people present to meet them. Most of these conventions were held in the open country, as most of the Danish churches were

129

rural churches. At the station all were loaded into buggies and driven to the church. There a committee sent groups to homes where they would live during the meeting. Frequently there were more than a hundred guests for such a convention.

Saturday morning all were up early and had breakfast on the farm. The meeting began at nine and frequently some people had a long way to drive. The meeting opened with devotions which were in charge of one of the pastors. The rest of the morning could be used for the business of the district organization. Officers were elected, and among other things it was decided which speakers were to visit the different societies during the coming year.

At noon all the guests and many of the local people ate their meal in the church basement or in a nearby hall.

After the meal, the young people played singing games. The meeting began again at two. The first thing on the program was a talk by one of the leaders. It was usually one of the pastors from the district who spoke. Pastor Hoiberg was always a favorite. At this meeting they sang Danish songs as a rule.

After this meeting came the gymnastics tournament. There could be three or four competing teams. There were judges and the winning team won a banner on which was inscribed in bold letters, in Danish: ALTID HØJERE (Always Higher).

There was considerable interest in this tournament. The teams from the different societies put on their exhibition one at a time. There were usually three judges. With pad and pencil in hand, they walked about quietly. Usually the contests were held in a hall, but if the audience was too large, they were held outside. The spectators cheered and clapped when things were done well. Gymnastics were so common in Danish circles that people had a pretty good idea when exercises were done well.

When the teams had finished their exhibitions, the judges met and reached an agreement as to the winning team. One was selected to be the spokesman and would

130

give a little talk and announce the winner. He then got the banner, and asked the leader of the winning team to step forward and he presented the banner to this team. If a team won the banner three times in succession, it became the property of that team.

After the contest, there were plays and games again. These lasted till supper.

Saturday evening could be spent in different ways. Some times there was a talk. Quite often the local society presented a home talent play. For many years these were Danish plays. As we moved farther into the twentieth century, the plays were more often American. One question aroused some controversy and that was whether or not there should be a dance with a band at these conventions. There was considerable opposition. Some were held, however.

On Sunday morning at ten, there were church services. This was well attended, and it was often difficult to find a seat in the church. The services were always in the Danish. Frequently, there was a communion service too.

Sunday dinner was the big dinner. The host society did its best to have the tables beautifully decorated with flowers, greenery and flags, both American and Danish. The food, too, was their best, and these farm people had a lot of it.

When all had eaten, there was a pause for visiting. Following this there was often an exhibition of folk dancing. There were no judges. Each fellow was a judge of the pretty girls who danced, and their ancient costumes were also an attraction. The different dances were applauded heartily.

Following the folk dancing there was another meeting where usually one of the more popular speakers spoke. It was not easy to find a hall large enough to accomodate the audience so the meeting was often held in the church.

After this meeting, there were plays and games again. The young seemed to enjoy these immensely.

The evening meeting was the closing meeting. This was a short meeting. After this all the people gathered in the hall for a cup of coffee and a lunch. At the tables, there was much singing and good fellowship. There were talks of appreciation by representatives from each of the societies with many a thank you!

After this all went to their places of lodging to meet next day at the railway station. Here it was good-bye till the next convention.

The C. P. Hoiberg Tombstone at Nysted

XV
A NEW AGE COMING

The larger world was beginning to knock at the doors of this little Denmark in America. A new age was coming which would disrupt much and change more. The day of the modern world with its rapid transportation and communication was at hand.

About the turn of the century Rural Free Delivery came to our county. For some years, Jens Andersen had hauled the mail, twice a week, from Dannebrog to Nysted. Before the coming of daily mail there was no point in having a daily paper. We had none. Most of our weekly papers were written in the Danish language.

Some days before the mail carrier made his first trip over the route, it was generally known that he would start the following Monday. His new wagon had been on display in Dannebrog, and there was much talk about this wonderful creation. Father had seen it in town, and was pleased with it. He told us all about it. It was enclosed so that the carrier could ride in solid comfort in the most inclement weather. On the sides of the vehicle were printed in bold letters: U. S. MAIL. If proof were needed, this was it. Civilization had come to the prairies.

On the Monday that the carrier was to make his first round, I asked mother for permission to go up to the corner where our mail box had been set. She consented. Since I did not know when he would arrive, I went so early that I could not miss him. There was our mail box bearing proudly the name: Rasmus Nielsen. I was excited at the thought of seeing this harbinger of progress. I was surprised and disgusted that other people were not out to see it. They had no imagination. I stood there alone. I looked up the road. When I saw a team coming, I was sure that this was our U. S. Mail, but each time I was disappointed. I kept looking up the road, waiting and hoping. I felt like crying. How long I stood there, I do not know. I was so sad to have missed anything so thrilling. It proved that he had passed before I arrived.

Not long after, father began to receive a daily paper from Omaha. It contained a strip of comics. Life was good.

Some time after we received daily mail, father announced one day that the telephone was coming to our community. This was a wonder of wonders. One could talk over a wire, and that to people far away. Father had been in town and the manager of the newly formed company had asked him if he would take the telephone if a line came past his farm. Father was pleased with this attention. He told him that he would. We children became wildly enthusiastic, but mother did not say much. I don't think she thought it was very important. Not many weeks afterwards the linemen built the line past our farm. I followed the men as they dug the holes for the posts, and was deeply thrilled as they strung the wires. Father had told us that it was dangerous to touch the wires, and it was generally believed in our community that when a message went over the wires, the electric shock would kill any birds that chanced to sit on them.

The day came when the telephone was installed. We boys found it on the wall when we returned from our work. It was a marvelous apparatus, with a box near the top for complicated machinery. On the right side of the upper box was a crank, streamlined to reduce wind resistance. There was another box below which contained some mysterious things called batteries. The receiver was suspended on a hook from the left side, and the speaking transmitter was on an adjustable shaft midway from top to bottom. The whole thing had eye appeal. The wood was painted in a

134

delicate golden oak color, while the metal was a shining black trimmed with nickel.

After we had finished our evening chores, we had time to behold and study this new work of genius. The girls had been instructed in the use of it, but this proved a bit confusing. They said our call was three rings. But how were we to know when we were wanted, as there was an assortment of three rings. There was a long and two shorts, two longs and a short, one short and two longs, two shorts and one long or just three shorts. This was indeed confusing! Well, the girls insisted that our ring was just simply three rings, and we answered every time there were three rings. But everybody else on the party line answered when there were three rings, so there was a bewilderment of hellos.

We also had some difficulty in putting in a call. The girls had understood that we had to call Central and ask for our party, and then hang up till she notified us. The result was that it took several days to get a party. It was quicker to carry a message on foot than by phone. But we finally learned. When we put in a call we were very specific. Since no number was assigned to any telephone, we called by name and gave any further information or description that would help in locating the party. In calling our nearest neighbor we said, "Central, please give me J. C. Jensen out in the country." Since the Jensens were on our line, we had to hang up the receiver, while Central did the ringing.

In those days the telephone was truly a means of disseminating information. There were many parties on our line, and when a person talked, he could be certain of an attentive audience. There was no heckling. If one wanted a third party to join the conversation, all that had to be done was to ask her to join it. As a rule, she did that promptly. We could talk all over the county, and before long all over the state, then over the nation and finally all over the world.

One summer evening my brother, Chris, and I drove to Dannebrog to see a tent show. I have long since forgotten what the tent show was about. But after the first show, I saw something I have not forgotten. Before the last act of the first show, a barker came around telling us about something really wonderful. It was called Moving Pictures. This show would follow the first show and if we missed it we would miss half of our lives. I was thoroughly interested and already enthusiastic, but there was one serious drawback and that was that I had no money. This was nothing new. In my distress, I turned to my brother and asked him if he was going to let this chance of a lifetime slip by. He replied that he might stay on to see it. I told him of my financial predicament. He did not seem surprised and lent me a quarter, and we saw our first movie.

The name of the picture was **Bold Bank Robbery.** There was much flickering and the film broke several times. But we had seen something. Not only had we seen how robbers rob a bank, but we had proof that justice triumphs over wrong. As we drove from town in our cart that night, we did not talk about the first show, but about the moving picture. We did not know that we had seen something that would change civilization, but we did know that we had seen something that was exciting. I got my quarter's worth.

I don't remember the first automobile I saw or when I saw it, but I do remember my first ride in a car. It was at the September Eighth Festival at Nysted. There were many people present and during the noon hour, an agent from St. Paul came out to demonstrate his car. It was a bright and shining thing with a top that could be raised and lowered. On this beautiful, late summer day, the top was down. He gave several people a ride. Once when he came back, four of us young fellows pushed our way up to the car. The driver must have seen our eager faces, for he said, "Jump in, boys." We needed no urging. We were in and he drove us around Section Five, telling us what a marvelous thing it was. I believed every word.

The first long trip I took came not so long after. There was a young people's convention in Denmark, Kansas. Many of the young people from Nysted were planning to attend, but railway connections to Denmark were not good. One Sunday we were with Harry and Thomas S. Hermansen, and the latter said half in jest, "Why don't we hire a car and driver and go down there in automobile?" This was certainly an interesting idea, but we were agreed that the cost would be entirely too high. However, after talking back and forth about the matter for some time, it was agreed that Tom should talk to a Mr. Clausen in Dannebrog. He sold cars and he might be interested in making the trip.

Some days later Tom came down to our place and reported that Mr. Clausen would drive the four of us the two hundred miles to Denmark and back for fifty dollars. He would buy the necessary gasoline and oil, and take care of any needed repairs. We, however, would have to take care of his board and lodging costs at the three-day meeting. Considering the cost of railway transportation, and after having consulted with our parents, we came to the conclusion that the price was fair and that we would accept the offer. We notified him that his offer had been accepted, and that we would come to Dannebrog and be ready to set out at the hour of nine on a certain Thursday. Mr. Clausen asked us to take care of such details as to which road to take. There were no marked highways. We agreed to do it. We had on old geography in which there were rather large maps of Nebraska and Kansas. We made a list of the chief towns between Dannebrog and Denmark.

On the day we had agreed to set out, father took Chris and me to Dannebrog. We had the geography with us, just in case we got lost. Mr. Hermansen took Tom and Harry to town. They arrived at about the same time we did. Each of us boys had an old suitcase for our best clothes. We travelled light in those days.

Mr. Clausen was a little late, so we did not get started till nine-thirty a. m. He drove an Overland touring car. This was really adventure and we were a little impatient because of the late start.

We told Mr. Clausen that the first city to drive to was Grand Island. He knew the road to that city. In places there was deep sand and steep hills, but the car pulled well and we made it. When we came to Grand Island, we stopped at a garage, and asked the road to Hastings. There were no filling stations. We were told which roads to take and that it was about twenty-five miles south and west. We wrote down the directions and set out again. There were no hard surface roads, only dirt roads, and these were full of nails which had fallen from wagons and hayracks, so we had some punctures. Flat tires were part of the adventure.

At Hastings we again stopped at a garage, and asked for the road to Blue Hill. Once again we made notations of the directions. We had now driven about fifty miles and we decided to eat our noon day lunch. Hastings was one of the largest cities we would pass through.

We had no trouble to speak of in finding Blue Hill where we found a garage and asked about the road to Guide Rock.

As we drove south toward Guide Rock, we noticed that the corn was much better than it was at home. In fact it was so good that we asked Mr. Clausen to stop at a field so that we could pick some choice ears. We found several and we took them with us to the car. We thought it would be fun to pick such excellent corn. We reached Guide Rock which is not very far from the Kansas line. In this village we asked about the road to Mankato, Kansas.

It seemed that the Kansas roads were a little better than the Nebraska roads. Things were going well and we four fellows became silly. We amused ourselves and annoyed farmers whom we met by throwing shelled corn at them and their horses.

At Mankato we asked for the road to Beloit and when we arrived there, it threatened rain. We ate supper and when we had eaten, Mr. Clausen put the chains on the car, raised the top, and soon the rain fell.

From Beloit we drove south toward Victor. In the soft mud of the rich Kansas soil, we could drive but slowly. There were times when the car barely moved. We had to get out and push a time or two. We had planned to reach

138

Denmark that evening, but we did not make that. It was ten when we arrived at Victor. We drove up to a building and someone opened a window and shouted, "Are you looking for a doctor?" We told the voice that we were looking for a place to sleep. It told us that there was no hotel in town. We ended up sleeping in an old haymow. The hay was musty and the mice were active, but we slept the sleep of the young and tired.

Next morning we got up early. There was no place to wash and eat, so we drove on to Denmark. It was a slow drive through the Kansas mud. Once there our needs were taken care of.

There must have been at least one hundred fifty guests at this meeting. There was one automobile in addition to ours. It was from Cozad, Nebraska.

This meeting was like others that have been told about. We stayed with a family in Vesper, which was about ten miles from Denmark. So sticky were the Kansas roads that when it rained one day, rather than trying to get through the mud, we decided to stay in the hall near the Denmark church overnight. Other young fellows did the same. We got little sleep.

Our drive home was much the same as the one down to Kansas. In fifteen years or so, the car became so common that people drove from coast to coast.

XVI

CONCLUSION

The moving finger writes; and having writ,
Moves on: nor all the piety nor wit
Shall lure it back to cancel half a line,
Nor all the tears wash out a word of it.
                    —Omar Khayyam.

At the end of the first decade of this century, I left
Nysted and did not spend much time there after that. Now
that I have reached an advanced age, I like to look back at
the experiences of my childhood and youth.

When I was a boy, I often thought the sun shone a
little brighter on our community than upon other communities
in our county. I am sure that some of the old Danes felt
that these strangers lived in the great darkness. But the
outside world was knocking at our doors. More and more
young people went to the cities and came back with strange
clothes and stranger ideas. The young became conscious
of being "foreigners," and as that feeling grew they became
more and more reluctant to sing the Danish songs and hymns.
It was not considered patriotic. People who could not speak
Danish bought farms. The nations inter-married. Old
pioneers went to their eternal home. Little by little group
solidarity became weaker. Many co-operatives failed. The
folk school found it more and more difficult to get students.
Finally it closed and weeds grew where flowers had grown.

But that was not all. It almost seems that the Nysted
community, like Hiroshima, stood in the way of progress.
It was battered from all sides. Two forces struck it mighty

blows: one was the cruelest depression in American history, and the other was an eight-year drouth. What falling prices did not do, scorching southwest winds did. There were farm auctions and over the prairies were heard the cries, "sold, sold, sold." It was moving day every day, and the sons and daughters of proud pioneers piled what few things they had into old cars and drove off to cities.

The fate that overtook the Rasmus Nielsen farm was no exception. Some years ago, I walked across the fields to the old homestead. I had known every spot on this farm. A thousand memories crowded upon me as I walked over the once familiar ground. All the buildings except the house were gone. Our old home was a wreck, with gaping holes and smashed windows. I went to the very spot where we had stood so many times listening to the Christmas chimes from the Nysted church. For a moment, it seemed that I heard my mother's voice. The trees were gone. They did not pay. Bulldozers had been used to grub them out. The robins and the wrens sang no more. Where there had been much laughter and song, only the sigh of the Nebraska wind was heard. It was so empty.

I turned away. I crossed the well-known field. I looked over the Oak Creek valley. I saw more empty farm buildings. The moving finger had reached the end of a chapter.

Was this little Denmark a success? Yes, while it lasted. But it could not and should not last. Canada is a nation with two languages. The Swiss are so civilized that they can have four languages and still be a nation. But in America, we have all the nations of the world. We are the united nations. Our nation could not last with scores of languages. Even as this is written, our cohesion is not any too strong.

Many people think that such an alien pocket as Nysted was an evil. I think not. Strong enlightened citizens are an asset to any nation. Furthermore, we children, through our acquaintance wtih the cultural heritage of our parents, came to love it and them. We were spared the heartaches of so many immigrants and their children in our large cities. So often these children fail to see that their parents have anything of value. Their parents wear strange clothes and love queer things. Too often these children reject the cultural heritage of their parents and fail to discover the best in America.

When I reached the age of fourteen, I was familiar with, yes loved, many Danish songs, hymns and stories. My parents had social status in our community. Both father and mother were important people in our little world. I was proud of being their son. How I beamed when father or mother came to visit our school. When I accompanied father to a meeting of farmers and he stood up and expressed his frank opinion, it never occurred to me that it was wrong for him to do that in the Danish language.

The fact that I learned to speak Danish first, did not make it more difficult for me to learn the English. The fact that I learned to love good poetry and prose in the Danish, made it all the easier for me to appreciate Hawthorne, Whitman, Steinbeck and Edna St. Vincent Millay at a later day.